Southern Central America

W9-BWU-107

Nicoya

San Jose

PANAMA

COSTA RICA

Buenaventura

The Northern Andes

Quito

ECUADOR

Napo R.

COLOMBIA

Santa Marta

Caura River

Magdalena River

Bogota

Valencia

Caracas

VENEZUELA

Orinoco River

Amazon Region

Amazon River

MARAJAO

Santarem

Mirakanguera

The Central Andes

Maranon R.

Ucayali R.

Trujillo

Lima

PERU

Cuzco

Lake Titicaca

La Pa...

BOLIVIA

Madeira River

Tapajoz River

BRAZIL

ATACAMA

CHILE

The Southern Andes

ARGENTINA

Valparaiso

Santiago

Buenos Aires

Plata River

Frontispiece: Crown, 8½" high, with four plumes, 12⅝" high.
Collar, 17¼" long, with twenty-four pendants, each 3¼".
Two epaulettes, each 7" long, with six pendants, each 2¼".
Necklace with nine beads, 1⅞" diameter.
Two earplugs, 4⅞" diameter.
Gold. The only complete set of adornments used by a chieftain for ceremonial purposes.
Collection: Rafael Larco Hoyle, Chiclin, Peru

ANCIENT ARTS
OF THE ANDES

BY WENDELL C. BENNETT

WITH AN INTRODUCTION
BY RENÉ D'HARNONCOURT

THE MUSEUM OF MODERN ART   NEW YORK
IN COLLABORATION WITH
THE CALIFORNIA PALACE OF THE
LEGION OF HONOR, SAN FRANCISCO;
THE MINNEAPOLIS INSTITUTE OF ARTS

ACKNOWLEDGMENTS

On behalf of the Trustees of the Museum of Modern Art, the Director of the exhibition "Ancient Arts of the Andes" respectfully acknowledges a debt of gratitude to the Government of Peru and to General Juan Mendoza, Minister of Public Education of Peru, for the loan of outstanding works of art, and for generous cooperation in the preparation of the exhibition.

We are particularly grateful to His Excellency Señor Don Fernando Berckemeyer, Ambassador Extraordinary and Plenipotentiary of Peru, to Dr. George Muelle, Director of Archeology and History, Ministry of Public Education, Sra. Dra. Rebeca Carrión Cachot, Director of the Museo Nacional de Antropología y Arqueología, and to Sr. Julio Fernandez Davila, Consul General of Peru in New York.

For lending to the exhibition important collections that have never before been publicly shown or published, the Director wishes especially to thank Sr. Don Rafael Larco Hoyle, Chiclin, Peru, and Dr. Norbert Mayrock, Santiago, Chile.

Our sincerest gratitude and thanks also go to the following individuals and cooperating institutions for the loan of objects: American Museum of Natural History, New York; Art Institute of Chicago; Dr. Junius B. Bird, New York; Mr. Robert Woods Bliss, Washington, D.C.; The Brooklyn Museum; Carlebach Gallery, New York; The Cleveland Museum of Art; Dr. Joseph L. Costa, New York; Mr. Ernest Erickson, New York; Etnografiska Museet, Göteborg, Sweden; Mrs. Olga Anhalzer Fisch, Ecuador; Dr. James A. Ford, New York; Dr. Hans Gaffron, Chicago; Heeramaneck Galleries, New York; Mr. and Mrs. A. B. Martin, New York; Mr. George Hewitt Meyers, Washington, D.C.; The Minneapolis Institute of Arts; The Montreal Museum of Fine Arts; Mr. Charles Lucien Morley, New York; El Museo Nacional de Antropología y Arqueología, Peru; Museum für Völkerkunde, Munich, Germany; the Museum of the Cranbrook Academy of Art, Bloomfield Hills, Michigan; The Museum of the American Indian, Heye Foundation, New York; National Gallery of Art, Washington, D.C.; Chicago Natural History Museum; Peabody Museum, Harvard University; Mr. Nelson A. Rockefeller, New York; Sr. José Sabogal, Peru; Mr. Hugh Smith, New York; Miss Darthea Speyer, Paris, France; The Textile Museum, Washington, D.C.; Dr. Harry Tschopik, Jr., New York; The University Museum, Philadelphia, Pa.; Mr. John Wise, New York;

to Mrs. Gertrud Mellon, Mr. Nelson A. Rockefeller, and the Cleveland Museum of Art for contributing the color plates to this volume;

to Dr. René Batigne, Dr. Joseph O. Brew, Miss Geraldine Bruckner, Dr. E. K. Burnett, Mr. Donald Collier, Mr. Richard Davis, Dr. Heinrich Ubbelohde Doering,

Dr. Paul Fejos, Dr. A. V. Kidder, Dr. Andreas Lommel, Dr. Samuel K. Lothrop, Dr. Paul Martin, Mr. William M. Milliken, Mr. F. Cleveland Morgan, Mr. Charles Nagle, Mr. Frederick C. Orchard, Mr. Frederick Pleasant, Dr. Froelich Rainey, Mr. Meyric Rogers, Dr. Harry L. Shapiro, Dr. Mathew Stirling, Mr. William Duncan Strong, Dr. Luis E. Valcárcel, Miss Bella Weitzner, Mr. Gordon R. Willey, Mr. John Wise, for counsel and assistance in the assembling of the exhibition;

to Lee Bolten, Dr. Heinrich Ubbelohde Doering, Herbert Matter, Nickolas Muray, Pierre Verger, and Pocahontas Press for photographs;

to Pan-American Grace Airways and W. R. Grace and Co. for a generous financial contribution to the exhibition and for assistance in its assembly;

to Dr. Junius B. Bird for counsel in the assembly of the exhibition and guidance in the restoration of important objects;

to Sr. Augusto Alvarez Calderón for his assistance in the assembly of the Peruvian loans.

The Director of the exhibition especially wishes to thank Miss Mildred Constantine, who rendered valuable assistance on all phases of the preparation of the book and the exhibition.

R. D'H.

CONTENTS

INTRODUCTION

This book deals with the arts of the pre-Columbian civilizations of the Andes and with related arts from the adjacent Amazon region and southern Central America. Objects from the two latter areas are included only when they seem more closely tied to Andean influences than to Caribbean, Mayan or Mexican as the case may be.

As Wendell Bennett points out (p. 17) few sections of this vast area have been studied intensively enough by archeologists to enable them to establish reliable chronologies of style. Only in Peru have we enough data to know the relative age of the major cultures. The few studies that have been carried out in the northern Andes, Central America, and the Amazon region, are insufficient to correlate the styles of these sections with the Peruvian styles or with each other.

Under these circumstances it is often impossible to trace the direction of the flow of influences from one cultural center to the other throughout the Andean area. In some cases the kinship between two styles from distant regions seems obvious yet lack of knowledge makes it impossible to state whether these similarities are the result of migrations, of military or spiritual conquest, of trade, or of a common cultural background.

Another circumstance that makes the study of Andean art difficult is the scarcity of data on individual pieces. Many objects of artistic importance come to the attention of the scientist only after they have been in the possession of pot hunters, traders or private collectors who are unable or unwilling to give information on the exact place and circumstances under which the pieces were originally found.

While it is obvious that years must pass before an analytic study of the whole scope of Andean art can be undertaken, nevertheless a few conclusions can be drawn from evidence supplied by regional studies and by the objects themselves. It is already safe to say, for instance, that there is no common denominator for all the styles of the various Andean cultures, but that each is related to some of the others in style, technique, or subject matter in what might be called a network of Andean characteristics.

An interesting example of the wide distribution of one element of subject matter rendered in a specific style is the mouth of a feline with prominent incisors, which was used in carvings, metal work, pottery and textiles, all the way from Chile to southern Central America. The same subject also appears in Mexico, but the Mexican version with its peculiarly high arched lips seems unrelated to the Andean. The Andean feline mouth motif is the dominant element in the stone carvings of Chavín de Huántar, one of the oldest known religious centers of Peru. An excellent example of the importance of this motif in Chavín is the composite image of a monster from

Fig. 1. Drawing of composite image of a mythical monster from a carved stone stela. Chavín de Huántar, Peru

the monolith known as the Stela Tello (Fig. 1), on which the feline mouth can be found seven times as part of a feline or a human head and at least once as an isolated element. In other Chavín carvings it appears even on representations of birds where it intrudes as a continuation of the beak (Fig. 2). It is clear that this mouth is used in Chavín as a symbol rather than a representation of animal anatomy, and one may also conclude that it was meant to convey the idea of supernatural power and that its appearance on creatures unrelated to the cat family identified them as mythical beings. The frequent appearance of the motif at various times and in many regions of Peru, Bolivia, and northern Chile is indicative of the importance of Chavín as a fountain head of ritual art in the central and southern Andes. Figs. 33, 39, 79, and 82, illustrate this point. The motif is also found on objects from the northern Andes such as the stone carvings of San Agustín in Colombia (Fig. 157) and even on Central American goldwork like the plaques of Coclé in Panama (Fig. 184). In the last two cases, identity of subject matter and similarity of style are the only evidence that relates them to their Peruvian counterparts. We know nothing about the time necessary for the wide distribution of Chavín influence or the manner in which it was transmitted. To learn about the process of style distribution we must turn to more recent periods.

An unusually well documented example of the rapid distribution of an art style over a large area is seen in the spread of the Inca style during the expansion of the Inca Empire. At its greatest extent the Empire reached from what is now northern Chile to central Ecuador, a distance of well over two thousand miles. It included large population centers whose varied cultures had produced highly individual art forms of their own long before the relatively short period of Inca rule. But in the ruins of the old towns archeologists have found pottery of local make in typical Inca shapes, with characteristic Inca designs. The early Spanish chroniclers tell us that the totalitarian Inca Empire had a well defined policy for incorporating newly conquered peoples into the state. They were forced to accept not only the Inca's political and religious systems but even such details as their manner of dress, and the entire production of crafts for ceremonial use and for the nobility was put in the hands of state employed specialists.

It is unlikely that the distribution of earlier styles in the Andean area followed such a rigid pattern as in the case of the Incas. We may be sure that transmission of design was often the result of the more gentle processes of diffusion that come with social and ceremonial contacts and with trade. Only where early styles were transmitted in relatively unmodified form as in Tiahuanaco does it seem probable that we are dealing with the results of conquest and colonization.

The use of the same techniques in different regions and at different epochs is another factor that points to the interdependence of the various Andean cultures. Methods of pottery decoration like negative painting, in which the undyed portions of the surface constitute the design, are found throughout the northern and central Andes, as are many specific methods of metallurgy. One of the most striking characteristics of the high civilizations of Peru is their common emphasis on sheer excellence of technique, the more noteworthy since mastery of the various media is nowhere accompanied by evidence of mechanical inventiveness. Craftsman's tools such as looms, spindles, carving and polishing instruments were, without exception, of extremely simple construction and no efforts were made to facilitate the craftsman's work by labor-saving devices or mechanical guides to make accuracy easy. In spite of this, the great embroidered mantles of Paracas (Fig. 52), the fine ponchos of the Tiahuanaco period (Fig. 88), the paper-thin walls of certain ceramics from Paracas Cavernas and the giant stone masonry of the Incas are all demonstrations of ultimate perfection in technical skill. In the case of Incaic stone work we are still unable to understand how it was possible to fit the uneven contours of enormous stones with such precision that the chinks between them cannot be entered by a knife blade. Superb craftsmanship was in fact an essential element in architecture which relied for its effect not on ornament, but on the form of the structure, the pattern of the stone work and the sensitivity of its execution. The beauty of the great mantles of Paracas, with their infinite number of stitches and complexity of design, was also dependent on the application of the utmost skill; incredibly expert weaving was

Fig. 2. Drawing of a condor, from a stone frieze. Chavín de Huántar, Peru

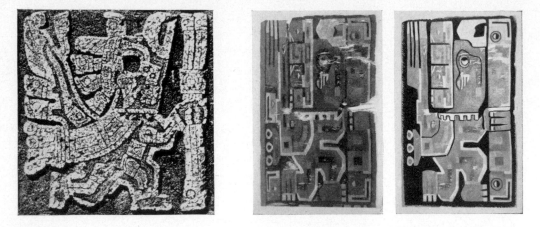

Left: Fig. 3. Stone relief of human figure with condor head. Detail from the "Gate of the Sun" of Tiahuanaco, Bolivia. *Right:* Fig. 4. (a) Detail from Coast Tiahuanaco textile; (b) Same detail as at left, with background of figure blacked out

needed to preserve order in patterns so involved that they could easily have become chaotic if they had been executed without great precision.

While it would be difficult to find anywhere in the world standards of technical excellence to match those of Peruvian ceramics and textiles, in certain types of work such as the quantity production of elaborately decorated ceramics typical of the later phases of Peruvian art standardization of skill seems to have produced a conflict between quality of execution and quality of design. Looking at a large number of such vessels one is often struck by their monotony in spite of the great variety of subject matter used in the decoration. The designs seem to have been put together according to established formulas rather than by spontaneous reaction to an artistic problem. Spontaneity is not a characteristic of late Peruvian art. This may be due to the passion for organization that we know was present in Inca civilization and suspect was present in some of the preceding cultures. If this is true it may explain why early Peruvian objects like the Paracas mantles, whose creation gave artists both the necessity and the pleasure of using all their extraordinary capacity for long careful planning, are the ones that in turn give us the greatest delight.

Modern artists and people concerned with modern art who have shown great interest in Negro Africa, Oceania, and pre-Columbian Mexico have so far paid relatively little attention to Andean work, probably because its finest and most original examples are still little known to anyone but the professional archeologist. The pieces most frequently seen in the public collections of Europe and North America belong to the late Peruvian civilizations and lack, as a rule, the vigor and originality of the earlier art. The discovery of the work of the early civilizations is of relatively recent date and since exportation is prohibited very few fine examples can be seen

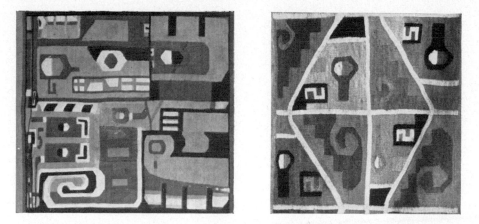

Left: Fig. 5. Detail of a poncho. Coast Tiahuanaco, Peru. 21″ long. Collection: Nelson A. Rockefeller, New York. *Right:* Fig. 6. Detail of a poncho. Coast Tiahuanaco, Peru. Collection: Dr. Eduard Gaffron Collection, courtesy The Art Institute of Chicago. See also Fig. 91

outside Peru. The ceramic sculpture of the Northern Andes, which includes some of the most interesting objects, is even less accessible than that of the early Peruvian cultures.

An effort has been made in this book to illustrate some fine examples from all these regions and from the known major periods that produced outstanding work, and it might be of interest to comment on certain aspects of this art that recall the esthetic problems of our time or shed light on the processes of art itself.

The various degrees and kinds of "abstraction" that are typical of Tiahuanaco, are a case in point. Fig. 3 is a stone relief from the "Sun Door" in Tiahuanaco. It represents a very popular subject of Tiahuanaco art, a running human figure with the head of a condor. Fig. 4a is a tapestry of the same subject done in a geometric style that makes it nearly impossible to recognize the subject. In Fig. 4b the background of the tapestry has been blacked out for us so that the running bird-man can again be recognized. If Figs. 3 and 4 are carefully compared, it will be seen that the seemingly abstract weaving actually retains every major element of the realistic stone carvings.

Fig. 5 is another favorite subject of Tiahuanaco, a profile view of a jaguar taken from a tapestry poncho. Fig. 6 represents the same feline but this time most of the elements that compose Fig. 5 have been omitted so that only the eye, the teeth, and the tail of the animal remain.

Both the textiles shown in Figs. 4 and 6 are seemingly abstract patterns developed from realistic images, but the processes of abstraction used in the two cases are radically different. The first was achieved by conventionalizing every element in the original design, the second by omitting all but those elements deemed necessary to

Left: Fig. 7. Jar in shape of a man carrying a dog. Mochica, Peru. Clay, 8″ high. Collection: Peabody Museum, Harvard University. (46.77.30/4974) *Right:* Fig. 8. Jar in shape of a seated man holding a rattle. Santarem, Brazil. Clay, 17″ high. Collection: University Museum, Philadelphia. (L-109-1) See also Figs. 207 and 208

make the subject matter recognizable. Since the second process used the already conventionalized forms of the first, it must be assumed that it is a later development.

Another process that led to abstraction was the transformation of the natural caves of Machu Picchu and Kenko into Inca ceremonial centers. To make it possible to use these caves for ceremonial purposes, passages had to be widened, ceilings strengthened by stone masonry, and altars and seats carved into the living rock. But careful study of the caves reveals that the Inca went far beyond these functional modifications. They carved the ceilings and walls and rock buttresses into powerful geometric forms until the caves turned into abstract sculptures that enclose the visitor in hauntingly beautiful space (Fig. 124).

The Andean area produced many works of art whose subject matter was almost completely transformed into abstract design but it also produced some of the world's most realistic imagery. It is fascinating to see how the various treatments of one subject altered its meaning along with its appearance, particularly in the case of the pottery vessels representing human beings of which we have such a great quantity and variety. Among the Mochica of Peru (Fig. 7), a realistic human figure becomes a vessel merely by being made hollow and in some cases supplied with a spout. The

Left: Fig. 9. Vessel in shape of a seated man. Chancay, Peru. Clay, 16″ high. Collection: American Museum of Natural History. (B/8365) See also Fig. 95. *Right:* Fig. 10. Urn with human features. Chimborazo region. Clay. Collection: Olga Anhalzer Fisch, El Folklore, Quito

Carchi urn (Fig. 10), on the other hand, is a vessel made human by the application of a few light lines indicating nose, arms, necklace, and earrings. The ceramics from Santarem in Brazil (Fig. 8), and from Chancay in Peru (Fig. 9), represent other moments in this progression from human figurine with ritual use and meaning to vessel with ritual life. The works dealt with in this book cannot begin to give a complete representative picture of Andean art, but it is hoped that they will convey an idea of its scope and quality and by so doing serve as an incentive to further studies.

RENÉ D'HARNONCOURT

Fig. 11. Stela Bennett. Tiahuanaco, Bolivia. Nearly 24′ high. This monolithic statue, discovered by Wendell C. Bennett in 1932, is a superb example of representational sculpture, retaining the strength and dignity of the column from which it was carved.

The death of Wendell C. Bennett in the summer of 1953 was a great loss to American archeology. Dr. Bennett was Chairman of the Department of Anthropology of Yale University and recognized as one of the foremost authorities on the ancient civilizations of South America. The Museum of Modern Art wishes to acknowledge its debt to a great scholar who gave us, in this book, prepared especially for this exhibition, an abstract of his life-work on Andean research.

R.D'H.

THE ANDES

Several distinctive culture patterns existed in the continent of South America at the time of its discovery by the Europeans following 1492. The rich pampas of Argentina and the plains of Patagonia were occupied by bands of nomadic hunters who pursued the guanaco and the American ostrich and gathered wild roots and seeds. The vast stretch of tropical forest in Amazonia was dotted with the thatched hut villages of warlike savages whose women cultivated corn, peanuts, and manioc and whose men hunted and fished and prepared for trophy-seeking raids on their neighbors. Only in the Andean mountains did the Spaniards encounter settled farming populations, advanced in technological achievement and in political and religious organization.

Many advanced civilizations had been built up in different parts of the highland Andes and the adjacent Pacific coastal plains, but although these shared a common cultural basis and exchanged ideas, they were never finally united into a single political system until incorporated as parts of the Spanish Colonial Empire. However, the Inca had gone far in building an extensive empire before the arrival of the Spaniards, and in earlier times, kingdoms of some magnitude had existed.

Archeology furnishes a basis for some broad divisions of the Andean cultures into a space and time framework. The Central Andes division encompasses the mountains and the Pacific coast of modern Peru with some extension into highland Bolivia. This area was closely united culturally throughout its known history, although political unity was achieved only slightly before the Spanish Conquest. The "South" refers to the Andean region of northwest Argentina and Chile, where past culture development had many parallels to that of the Central Andes but was essentially independent. The "North" includes the mountain regions of modern Ecuador, and Colombia, with extensions into Panama, Central America, and parts of Venezuela. The "East" covers the Amazonian tropical forest which had a cultural development all its own, although not totally unrelated to the Andean.

Long-term time sequences have been tentatively established only in the Central Andes, where six major time periods can be outlined within the span of the advanced civilizations. For the North and the South, certain widespread distributions of styles or techniques allow the assignment of some cultures to time periods corresponding to those of the Central Andes. However, many of the cultures must be left "floating" in time until further work has been accomplished.

The Andean mountain chain stretches in an elongated S-shaped curve down the western margin of the South American continent from Panama in the north to Tierra del Fuego in the south, a distance of over 3500 miles exclusive of the northwestern branch into Venezuela. These are formidable mountain barriers, from 100 to 400 miles in width, with many snow covered peaks over 20,000 feet in altitude, and with few passes under 12,000 feet. The Andes crowd close to the Pacific Ocean, leaving only narrow coastal plains, crossed by numerous, fast flowing mountain streams. On the eastern side, however, the tributaries of the Amazon originate within 100 miles of the Pacific, dash rapidly down to the tropical plains and meander peacefully to the Atlantic some 3000 miles away.

The narrow plains along the Pacific show greater environmental contrasts than do the high Andes. In the north, where altitude becomes the dominant climatic factor, the coasts of Colombia and northern Ecuador lie in the heart of the tropics and are covered with heavy jungle, while the coast of Peru is a desert. The only inhabitable parts of the desert are the flatlands along the rivers which originate in the Andes and cut their way to the Pacific. The coastal dryness increases in intensity to the south reaching a maximum in the Atacama desert of north Chile where rainfall has yet to be recorded. Further south, the central valley of Chile enjoys a Mediterranean climate quite similar to that of California.

The general geographical description of the Andes gives the impression that it would be a forbidding place indeed for the development of high civilizations in the past. However, in spite of the contrasting climates and the difficulties of mountain transportation, there are many compensating factors. The large structural highland basins have relatively rich soils, ample supply of water, and are generally free of forests or deep rooted grasses which would make cultivation difficult. The neighboring coastal valleys, once knowledge of irrigation allowed controlled distribution of the water supply, constitute rich agricultural areas. In the Central Andes, the absence of forests means that wood is not available for building or fuel but, on the other hand, stone is abundant and clays suitable for making sun-baked adobe bricks are found everywhere. There are also excellent clays for the potter; wool for the weaver from the llamas, the alpacas, and the wild vicuñas; grasses and reeds for the mat and basket makers. Furthermore, the Andes are everywhere rich in minerals: gold and platinum in the north; copper, gold and silver in the center; tin and copper in the south.

THE CENTRAL ANDES

The Central Andes include the coast and mountains of Peru and extend into the highland of Bolivia. They are bounded on the north by a long stretch of desert coast and a sparsely settled mountain range; on the east by the tropical Amazonian forests; and on the south by the Atacama desert which transverses the Andes. Within this area, the prehistoric civilizations had considerable cultural unity for approximately two thousand years before the Inca. This does not imply that the peoples of the Central Andes were totally isolated from the rest of the continent and, indeed, cultural influences both on and from the neighboring areas are often seen. However, the civilizations within the Central Andes, at any specific time period in the past, shared more with each other than they did with their neighbors to the north, east, and south.

Subsistence in the Central Andes was based on intensive agriculture, supplemented by herding in the mountains and by fishing on the coast. The basic plants and animals were known everywhere. Although some of these were environmentally limited, such as llamas, alpacas, and potato to the highlands, cotton, corn, and sweet manioc to the coast, all were distributed by trade. For example, coastal textiles have highland wools and highland plants are faithfully modeled on coastal ceramics. Cultivation techniques and implements were much the same: the latter including digging sticks, clod crushers, and hoes; the former, irrigation, terracing, crop rotation, and the use of fertilizer. The narcotic coca was chewed with lime and tobacco was unimportant.

The standard clothing comprised woven, untailored breech clouts, skirts, slit-neck shirts, shoulder shawls, head bands, and carrying bags with shoulder straps. Everywhere emphasis was placed on the crafts of ceramics, metallurgy, basketry, and weaving, although regional styles were distinctive and technological advances occurred in different time periods. Buildings were made of permanent materials, such as stone in the highlands, adobe on the coast, and there were always some massive constructions for religious or public purposes.

The population was concentrated in villages and there was always some political organization above the village units. The quantity of luxury goods produced implies that there was an abundance of leisure time over and above subsistence activities. There is also indirect evidence for the antiquity of group work patterns. Everywhere great emphasis was placed on burial which usually included elaborate and specially manufactured grave furniture.

SPATIAL DIVISIONS

The major subdivisions in the highlands are relatively easy to determine since there are only five structural intermont basins in the Central Andes suitable for maintaining large agricultural populations. These are, from north to south: the Cajamarca basin around the town of the same name; the Callejón de Huaylas which is drained by the highland branch of the Santa River; the Mantaro basin, inland from Lima, famed for its copper mines and the great weekly market at Huancayo; the Cuzco basin, center of the Inca Empire; and the Titicaca basin, which lies between Peru and Bolivia, and contains the largest lake in the Andes. Each of these basins has its distinctive culture history and each is still a center of population concentration.

Some twenty-five major rivers originate in the mountains and cut their way across the coastal plains to the Pacific. Each is separated from the next by desert stretches and mountain spurs, but in some sections several adjacent coastal valleys share enough cultural similarities to justify treating them as a group. At present, three groups of valleys can be considered as valid cultural units but the remaining ones must await future archeological work before being assigned to one of these three or set up as new units. A North Coast group includes the valleys of Chicama, Moche, and Viru, and was the center of the Mochica and the later Chimu civilizations. A Central Coast group covers the valleys of Supe, Chancay, Ancón, Rimac, and Lurín, all in the general neighborhood of the Peruvian capital of Lima. A South Coast group includes the valleys of Pisco, Ica, and Nazca, and is noted for its excellently preserved textiles, particularly those of the Paracas and Nazca civilizations. (See map, p. 185.)

Each of the highland basins and coastal valley units has certain local characteristics which persist through various time periods and stylistic changes. For example, the North Coast cultures all feature mold-made ceramics, modeling, and the stirrup-spout vessel; the South Coast emphasizes textiles and polychrome ceramic painting; and the Callejón de Huaylas shows a preference for multi-storied stone buildings, stone carving, and negative-painted ceramics. At the same time, each of these regions reflects the major stylistic and technological trends of the over-all culture history.

TIME DIVISIONS

The Central Andean civilizations have gross limits in time as well as in space. The terminal date is usually considered to be 1532 when the Spanish Conquest was initiated, although it is well recognized that this did not totally eradicate the Indian culture which has persisted up to the present day. The beginning date is harder to establish but should correspond to the time of the first appearance of such major characteristics of high civilization as agriculture, herding, ceramics, metallurgy, weaving, and building. At present, the date of approximately 1200 B.C. is assigned to this. Within this over-all time span, six major periods have been established, although some students prefer more, others fewer.

The problem of dating and matching regional sequences is far from being finally resolved. The ancient Peruvians not only lacked any form of writing but also any recorded calendars. Consequently, chronology is based on the relative dating techniques, and on the recently developed dating method using radio-active carbon.

Much of the archeological work has been devoted to the establishing of cultural sequences at a site or in a region. This can best be accomplished through the study

Fig. 12. Vessel in the shape of a feline with head-dress. Mochica. Clay. Collection: Museo Nacional de Arqueología y Antropología, Peru

of stratigraphy, namely, the superimposition of one cultural manifestation over another. This may involve the superimposition of one building on another, grave over grave, a building over a cemetery, a grave intrusive into a building platform, or the successive layers of refuse in an occupation site. Other relative dating techniques may be based on analysis of surface collections from many sites in a region, on the association of materials in graves, or on stylistic sequences. Virtually all of these techniques depend heavily on ceramics, since these are not only well preserved everywhere but also reflect successive styles.

The field excavations establish sequences for specific sites and these can often be matched to set up local or regional sequences. These regional sequences in turn can

Left: Fig. 13. Cup, decorated with feline motif that appears first in civilizations associated with Period One. Chavín. Stone, 4⅛″ high. Collection: Robert Woods Bliss, courtesy of the National Gallery of Art, Washington, D.C. (405) *Right:* Fig. 14. Bowl, illustrating the appearance of negative painting in Period II. Paracas Cavernas. Other styles from this culture are illustrated on pages 36-38. Clay. Collection: The Montreal Museum of Fine Arts. (48. AD. 31)

be matched with others through study of trade pieces, or by examination of certain styles and techniques which have spread from one section to another. Fortunately, Peruvian prehistory reveals many distinctive styles and techniques which diffused widely in comparatively short time. These are called "horizon" styles and are very useful in setting up broad relative sequences.

There have been various attempts to derive absolute dates from careful analysis of the Inca traditions, by comparative study of the thickness of refuse deposit in different periods, and by other such devices although none has been very satisfactory. The newly developed Carbon 14 method promises to furnish more accurate approximations of absolute dates through the measurement of the rate of disintegration of the radioactive carbon in organic matter, such as bone, wood, shell, and the like, from ancient deposits. Thus far, only a few Peruvian archeological specimens have been dated, so that a reliable chronology cannot be established. The available evidence has been utilized in the assigning of gross dates to the six periods of the Central Andes, but it must be noted that these are highly tentative, and may well be radically changed when more specimens have been dated. Certain characteristics of the art of these periods are shown in Figs. 13 to 18.

Period One (approximately 1200 to 400 B.C.) starts with the earliest appearance of ceramics on the North Coast of Peru, accompanied by corn, manioc, true weaving, and other elements. It does not represent the earliest known culture, however, since

Left: Fig. 15. Vessel in shape of a seated man. Mochica; an early example of realism from Period III. Clay, 11″ high. Collection: University Museum, Philadelphia. (39-20-11) *Center:* Fig. 16. Cup with painted decorations. Tiahuanaco, Period IV. The feline motif and the complexity of the somewhat geometric style recall the art of Period I. Clay, 8¼″ high. Collection: American Museum of Natural History. (41.1/3828) *Right:* Fig. 17. Vessel, surmounted by two men leading a llama. Chimu. Its style, found in Period V, is a continuation of Mochica realism with emphasis on slick virtuosity. Black pottery, 7½″ high. Collection: Dr. Eduard Gaffron, courtesy The Art Institute of Chicago

it was preceded on the North Coast by a long pre-ceramic occupation, showing incipient agriculture and weaving which dates back approximately to 3000 B.C. Period One cultures have been found also on the Central Coast and in two of the northern highland basins. All are linked together by the Chavín horizon style, characterized by a highly stylized feline design, which appears on stone carving, ceramics, bone carving, gold work, clay reliefs, and textiles. There is, however, no direct evidence for the migration of peoples from one area to another nor of wide political organization. Instead, the wide spread of the Chavín feline design suggests religious influence so that the period has been called "Cultist" by some, although it is more commonly referred to as the "Early Formative." The names of some of the local cultures of this period are Chavín, Cupisnique, Early Ancón, and Early Supe.

Period Two (approximately 400 B.C. to 400 A.D.) is called "Late Formative" by some and "Experimenter" by others, because of the numerous technological innovations in building materials, weaving techniques, ceramics, and metallurgy. Cultures assigned to this period are found in most of the subdivisions of the Central Andes and named locally, Salinar, Cavernas, Chancay White-on-Red, Huaraz White-on-Red, Chanapata, and Chiripa. Two horizon styles unite this period, both based on techniques of ceramic decoration. The first is characterized by white-on-red positive painting, the second by a two-color resist negative painting.

Period Three (approximately 400 to 1000 A.D.) marks the culmination of technological development in the Central Andes and has been called "Mastercraftsman," "Florescent," and "Regional Classic," all names reflecting the high craft development, the artistic achievements, and the regional limitations of the component cultures. Many of the finest artistic examples of ceramics and weaving yet found in the Central Andean region are assigned to this period, which includes such well-known cultures as Paracas Necropolis, Nazca, Mochica, Recuay, and Pucará.

Period Four (approximately 1000 to 1300 A.D.) is dominated by the pan-Peruvian spread of the complex of Tiahuanaco styles. This spread may represent actual conquest and an incipient empire, although this is uncertain, but at least it eclipses the early styles in virtually every region of the Central Andes.

Period Five (approximately 1300 to 1438 A.D.) is again characterized by regional cultural manifestations following the disruption of the Tiahuanaco expansion. Population centers are much larger and in fact approach city proportions. Some of the local culture names are Chimu, Chancay Black-on-White, and Ica.

Period Six is that of the Inca Empire which, by the best reconstruction of traditional records, initiated its expansion from Cuzco in 1438 and terminated with the Spanish Conquest in 1532.

This sketch of the regional and temporal subdivisions of the Central Andes is intended merely as a general setting for more detailed presentation of some of the specific cultural manifestations. No attempt has been made to include the multitude of names now used for prehistoric periods, sites, and cultures in Peru. Terminology needs serious revision but until that is accomplished the names used here are the commonest ones, if not always entirely appropriate or consistent.

Fig. 18. Beaker. Inca. A typical example of the severe geometric forms frequently found in Period VI. Gold, 2¾" high. Collection: Dr. Eduard Gaffron, courtesy The Art Institute of Chicago

CENTRAL ANDEAN CULTURES

ORIGINS

The earliest inhabitants of the Central Andes, like those elsewhere in South America, were the nomadic hunters, fishers, and gatherers who had pushed southward from North America through the Isthmus of Panama. Although Panama is the only overland route into South America, the possibility of early as well as later trans-Pacific migrations cannot be totally ignored.

The problem of the immigration of the earliest inhabitants of South America is a fascinating and puzzling one, but hardly more so than that of the origin of high civilization in the Andes. This involves the question of plant domestication, and as yet the centers where the common New World plants were first domesticated are far from established. Numerous centers have been suggested for different plants, including Asia, the high Andes, the plains of Paraguay, the tropical forest, and Central America.

The earliest archeological information on domesticated plants in South America comes from the mouth of the Chicama valley on the north coast of Peru where Junius Bird excavated large mound like occupation sites of early inhabitants who practiced some agriculture but had no ceramics. One mound, over 40 feet in height, represents many years of occupation, dated by the Carbon 14 method as roughly 3000 to 1200

Fig. 19. Prehistoric gourds, c. 1600 B.C., found in Huaca Prieta, Chicama Valley, North Peru. c. 4½″ diameter. Collection: American Museum of Natural History

B.C. The subsistence was based on fishing, supplemented by farming. The domesticated plants include squash, the bottle gourd, beans, chili pepper, and cotton. Pottery, as mentioned, was unknown and true weaving was rare although twined cotton fabrics were abundant. Mats, nets, and bark cloth were made as well as chipped stone tools. Cooking was apparently done by stone boiling, that is by heating stones and dropping them in water containers. The houses were rough, small, subterranean rooms covered with whale bone and the burials were in simple pits or in slightly vaulted tombs. The over-all picture is one of a small population living in a peaceful, uninterrupted fashion over a long period of time.

These early farming sites are of interest since they show the long, slow process of cultural development which anteceded the establishment of the advanced Central Andean civilizations. It is by no means certain, however, that the more complex cultures which follow, on the North Coast of Peru and elsewhere, were a direct outgrowth of these humble beginnings. Indeed, the evidence from Chicama valley shows a sharp transition from the early farmers to the next period in which maize, manioc, well-made ceramics, true loom weaving, gold work, and architecture come in almost simultaneously, suggesting, at least, a migration from some other part of the country. Once established, however, the advanced cultures continue to develop in an interrelated fashion up to the time of the Spanish Conquest. As outlined earlier, this prehistoric development is divided into six major time periods, which are next described in sequential order.

PERIOD ONE (APPROXIMATELY 1200 TO 400 B.C.)

Local cultures pertaining to the first period have been found on the Central and North Coasts of Peru and in the Callejón de Huaylas and Cajamarca basins in the highlands. There is no evidence that these widely distributed local cultures were united politically but there may have been some religious unity since the highly stylized feline design, so characteristic of the highland ceremonial center of Chavín de Huántar, appears everywhere as a typical design motif.

CHAVÍN

The site of Chavín de Huántar lies to the east of the Callejón de Huaylas basin across the Cordillera Blanca, in a small river valley, a tributary to the Marañón. The valley is narrow and flanked on both sides by high mountain ridges. Landslides are not infrequent, and in fact a serious one in recent years covered over most of the Chavín

Opposite left: Fig. 20. Stela Raimundi. Found in Chavín de Huántar, Peru. An extremely formal carving of the feline deity, with a huge headdress consisting of cat-like faces and snake heads. Stylistically, the Stela Raimundi is a forerunner of certain Nazca designs (see Fig. 68). Carved stone slab, 6′ high. Collection: Museo Nacional de Arqueología y Antropología, Peru. *Opposite right:* Fig. 21. Carved monolith known as the "Lanzón" (spear), located in Chavín de Huántar. A landslide covered the site in 1945, but a cast is preserved in the Museo Nacional de Arqueología y Antropología, Peru. 15′ high

Fig. 22. Carved head of a snake, from the outer wall of the main structure in Chavín de Huántar. Stone. Collection: Rafael Larco Hoyle, Chiclin, Peru

ruins. Today the population of the valley is small and there is no reason to believe that it was materially larger in the past. Nonetheless, this isolated valley contains the ruins of the most elaborate center of the first period, that of Chavín culture.

The site is composed of a number of construction units arranged in a somewhat symmetrical pattern. A square, sunken court, about 157 feet on a side, is flanked on the north and south by high, stone-faced platforms, and on the west by a raised terrace which serves as the base for the principal building, called the Castillo. Other platform-like constructions lie to the north of the Castillo and there are numerous smaller units scattered about.

The Castillo is an impressive building, some 250 feet square and over 45 feet high, faced with dressed-stone slabs. The walls, pitched inward to compensate for the height, are set back near the top. Near the upper edge is a projecting cornice of dressed slabs decorated with carved feline designs, and under this a row of carved stone human and animal heads set on tenons inserted in the wall. The external appearance of the Castillo is that of a great solid block, but actually the interior is a honeycomb of three floors of galleries, rectangular rooms, and squared ventilation shafts. Ramps and stairways connect one floor with another, but there are no windows, and only hidden doorways leading to the outside. Most of the interior passages are barren, but in one intersection, where two galleries cross, stands a great prismatic stone, carved with deep grooves into the form of a feline monster. Startling indeed is this "Lanzón" when it is suddenly revealed in the darkened gallery by the flickering light of a candle or the beam of a torch.

No cemetery or burials have been found at this site, and the ceramic fragments encountered in excavations are quite drab compared to the architecture and the stone

Fig. 23. Mortar in shape of a puma, with characteristic surface decorations. Chavín de Huántar. Stone, 6½″ high. Collection: University Museum, Philadelphia. (SA 4627)

carving. The fragments are of shallow open bowls with thick rims, and simple collar jars. The ceramics were reduced fired to black, dark brown, and dark red colors and decorated with simple incisions, punched circles, stamped geometric designs, and, rarely, red painted areas outlined with incisions.

It is the stone carving which is most characteristic and which defines the Chavín style. Carving in the round is largely limited to the animal and human heads with projecting tenons for wall insertion, although there are also carved puma bowls, and other smaller artifacts. Flat carving is represented by wide and narrow stelae, like the now famous Raimondi stone, and by the incised slabs used as cornices. The carving is in low relief, achieved by incisions and cutting away of background in champlevé technique. Curved lines and bands predominate and there is a tendency to cover all of the available surface.

The stone carving design is thoroughly dominated by the stylistic representation of the feline. Even if the carvings represent other creatures certain characteristics of the feline can always be detected in them. The identifying characteristics of the feline are a wide mouth band which curves up at each end; crossed fangs; rows of small, squared teeth; a circular nose; an oval eye with cut-out notch at the top; and curved whisker

29

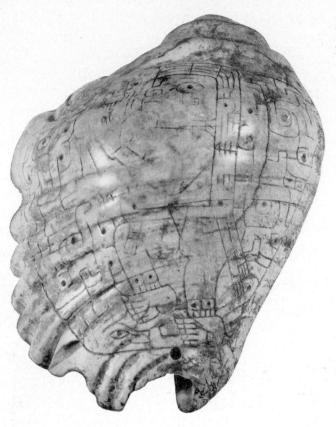

Fig. 24. Engraved shell. Chavín de Huántar. Collection: Mr. and Mrs. A. B. Martin, courtesy The Brooklyn Museum. (L.52.1)

bands. These features appear, with only minor variations, in the full figure, however portrayed, and in the detail units. For example, a feline head design unit is usually found on the collar, headdress, and tail, and at the ankle, elbow, and other joints of a figure. No other pre-Columbian culture shows such an overwhelming predilection for a single pervasive design motif.

The valley in which Chavín de Huántar is located could not have supported any large permanent population and in spite of the quantity of architectural remains, there is nothing to suggest extensive habitation. Instead the buildings appear to be temples and Chavín as a whole suggests a ceremonial center. If, like the contemporary town of Copacabana in Bolivia, it was a center at which religious pilgrims from many parts of the country assembled each year for a two to three week ceremony, this might account for the quantity of building and might also explain the wide spread of the symbolic Chavín feline design.

The first-period cultures elsewhere in the highlands and on the coast are not as elaborate as Chavín de Huántar. Some are represented only by thick refuse deposits, others by small temples made of rough stone and adobe, with thick clay plastered walls which are decorated with relief carving. The Cupisnique graves in Chicama valley contain thick stirrup-spout vessels and modeled figure jars as well as a great variety of

Above left: Fig. 25. Stirrup-spout jar, decorated with feline motif. Cupisnique. Its massive proportions are typical for this period. Clay. Collection: Museo Nacional de Arqueología y Antropología, Peru. *Above right:* Fig. 26. Stirrup-spout jar, in strong simple form, with engraved decorations. Cupisnique. Clay. Collection: Rafael Larco Hoyle, Chiclin, Peru

Below left: Fig. 27. Stirrup-spout jar, in shape of a seated man. Cupisnique. Clay. Collection: Rafael Larco Hoyle, Chiclin, Peru. *Below right:* Fig. 28. Stirrup-spout jar, in the form of a snake. (Spout is broken.) Cupisnique. Clay. Collection: Rafael Larco Hoyle, Chiclin, Peru

Fig. 29. Feline mask in Chavín style. Pachacamac. Silver, 8″ high. Collection: American Museum of Natural History. (B9450)

small bone ornaments and spatulas. Each of these cultures is on approximately the same technological level but otherwise independent. The unity with Chavín, as so frequently stated, is through the constant representation of the feline design. It appears on the carved clay wall of the Nepeña temples, on tapestry fragments from the shell heaps of Ancón, on carved bone and stirrup-spout vessels in Chicama, and on relief hammered gold in Lambayeque, far to the north. This wide spread of a specialized design reinforces the concept of a ceremonial center, visited by pilgrims who returned to their local communities inspired by the powerful, feline divinity.

Fig. 30. Crown of repoussé gold showing the feline deity flanked by two birds of prey. Chavín style. 12″ long. Collection: Rafael Larco Hoyle, Chiclin, Peru

Fig. 30A. Breastplate showing the characteristic Chavín-style combination of feline features and snake heads. Lambayeque. Gold, 4⅞″ high. Collection: The Cleveland Museum of Art, Dudley P. Allen Collection. (38.431)

33

SECHÍN

The site of Cerro Sechín in Casma valley is an exception. By all comparative evidence it belongs to Period One, but its unique stone carving is not in the Chavín tradition. This is even more puzzling since other places in the same valley are clearly Chavín influenced, like Moxeke with its row of high-relief clay figures surrounded with curled, feline-headed serpents.

Cerro Sechín is a large construction composed of two superimposed terraces. The lower one has a central stairway on each side of which are a series of upright facing slabs set at intervals. Each slab is carved in low relief with human figures, or parts of humans, like heads, bones, and vertebrae. Between the uprights are smaller blocks, each with a carved human face. Far from resembling Chavín, these upright figures are more suggestive of Los Danzantes at Monte Albán in far off Mexico. Cerro Sechín, then, is not only one of the rare coastal sites with stone carving, but also one that presents a new early style, thus far unrelated to other known Peruvian ones. Logically, it should be earlier than Chavín, but this has not been stratigraphically confirmed.

Fig. 31. Engraved slab from the Temple of Cerro Sechín. Of the known styles of Period I, that of Sechín is least related to Chavín. The feline motif is not dominant and the line is extremely free. Stone, c. 8′ high

Left: Fig. 32. Single-spout jar, with human figure connected with spout by flat bridge. Salinar. Clay. Collection: Rafael Larco Hoyle, Chiclin, Peru. *Right:* Fig. 33. Single-spout jar, with handle in the shape of a seated figure. Salinar. Clay. Collection: Rafael Larco Hoyle, Chiclin, Peru

PERIOD TWO (APPROXIMATELY 400 B.C. TO 400 A.D.)

The second period of cultural development in the Central Andes is characterized everywhere by experiments leading to technological controls. Irrigation systems are improved and the range of cultivated plants is enlarged. On the coast, walls are built of conical, ball-shaped, cylindrical, hemispherical, and rectangular adobes. New alloys appear in the metallurgy as well as new techniques of casting and gilding. Ceramics are oxidized fired, and both positive and negative painted. Each geographical subdivision supported its own local culture, without even the unification of a widespread stylized design. On the other hand, a new invention in one part soon spread to the others, and, as noted earlier, the two horizons which fall in this period are both based on techniques of ceramic decoration. Most of the local cultures are not particularly distinctive in their artistic production, although otherwise interesting, but two merit further description.

SALINAR

The Salinar culture on the North Coast of Peru is known largely from grave contents in ancient cemeteries in the Chicama valley. The ceramics have a wide range of shapes, of which the commonest are stirrup-spout containers, jars with spout and bridge to modeled figure, and tall bottles with cylindrical neck and single, flat handle. Some shapes and designs reflect the earlier Cupisnique culture, but the characteristic decoration is by modeling, incision, appliqué, and positive brush painting in white on

Fig. 34. Double-spout jar in shape of a trophy head, decorated with yellow, red, and green paint in areas outlined by engraved lines. Paracas Cavernas. Clay, 7½″ high. The walls of this jar are very thin — less than one-eighth of an inch. Its weight is about eight ounces. Collection: Norbert Mayrock, deposited at the Museum für Völkerkunde, Munich

a red base. Salinar is particularly noted for its small figure modeling on vessels. The graves also contain hammered gold pieces and carved bone spatulas, some of which preserve the Chavín design.

PARACAS CAVERNAS

On the South Coast, the isolated peninsula of Paracas lies just south of the Pisco valley. The peninsula is excessively dry and seemingly unfit for human habitation, but the excavations by Julio C. Tello in 1925 demonstrated that it was once an extensive burial ground. Tello distinguished two cultures at Paracas, one of which he named Cavernas, the other Necropolis. The Cavernas culture was considered the earlier one, and by relative matching it is assigned to the second period.

The Cavernas graves are deep chambers, either single or multiple, connected to the surface by cylindrical shafts, ten to twelve feet long and about five feet in diameter. The ceramics are again noted for variety of shapes including open bowls, dishes,

Fig. 35. Bowl decorated with geometric snake heads. Paracas Cavernas. Clay, 4½″ high. The change in direction of the two bands and the application of color provide a severely simple design with life and variety. Collection: University Museum, Philadelphia. (SA 3199)

Above left: Fig. 36. Figure of a flute-player; a very early representation of a person in an everyday pursuit. Paracas Cavernas. Clay, 8¾″ high. Collection: Dr. Junius B. Bird

Above right: Fig. 37. Small figurine with high hat. Paracas Cavernas. Clay, 3″ high. Collection: American Museum of Natural History. (641.0/8484)

Below right: Fig. 38. Circular object in the form of an animal head. Paracas Cavernas. Clay, 8¾″ diameter. Collection: The Montreal Museum of Fine Arts. (48.AD.32)

Fig. 39. Single-spout vessel in shape of feline holding a man. Viru. Pink clay, 8⅛″ high. Collection: Dr. James A. Ford

collar jars, bottles with flat handles, and containers with spout and bridge to modeled heads. Most of the vessels have a dark base color and are decorated by modeling, incision, appliqué, two-color negative painting, and a special type of post-fired painting in bright canary yellow, green, red, and black. The color areas are usually separated by incisions. Decorative designs are largely geometric but some of the incised designs bear a resemblance to the Chavín feline.

The Cavernas graves also contain baskets of totora reeds, some simple objects of gold, and great quantities of textiles woven in many different techniques. The finished fabrics show that the patterns of dress which characterize the Central Andes had been developed by this time.

Fig. 40. Stirrup-spout jar, representing a battle between magic bean warriors. Mochica. Clay, 10³⁄₁₆″ high. The style of Mochica painting is exceedingly fluid and light. It lends itself very well to conveying a sense of motion. Collection: Dr. Eduard Gaffron, courtesy The Art Institute of Chicago

PERIOD THREE (APPROXIMATELY 400 TO 1000 A.D.)

The long period of formation and experimentation culminated in the mastery of techniques and the establishment of flourishing culture centers in every major region of the Central Andes. The agriculturalists now possessed the total known range of Andean domesticated plants and animals, and cultivated almost every available acre by means of large-scale irrigation systems, terracing, and fertilizers. The crafts of ceramics, weaving, and metallurgy were among the best, technically and artistically, ever to be produced in pre-Columbian history. The architects directed the construction of large public works, and enormous temples. Quantities of luxury objects were produced for burial with the important dead. The populations were large and subjected to various types of social controls, both religious and political. Regionalism was marked, and each major area, which has been adequately examined, had its own distinctive cultural development. This does not mean that the regions were completely isolated since there is good evidence of trade in raw materials, military conflicts, and various other types of contacts. However, each local culture was capable of maintaining its own pattern in spite of the numerous influences from its neighbors.

Not all of the geographical regions of the Central Andes have been sufficiently studied for sound comparative work in this period. However, for the Mochica culture on the North Coast, the Paracas Necropolis and Nazca cultures on the South Coast, and the Recuay culture in the Callejón de Huaylas basin, there is ample evidence to show that each had its distinctive craftsmanship and design styles, and also that each presents a different pattern of cultural orientation.

MOCHICA

The Mochica culture was centered in the North Coast valleys of Chicama, Moche, and Viru but also extended to the valleys to the north and south. The archeological remains in each valley are quite uniform, suggesting a close cultural unity and at least incipient, over-all religious and political organization. However, the numerous battle scenes portrayed in the ceramic designs show conflicts between warriors of closely similar dress and weapons, which might indicate that political control was still not well enough established to prevent internecine warfare. On the other hand, it confirms other archeological evidence that the Mochica expansion was based on military conquest.

The Mochica is one of the best-known prehistoric cultures in the Central Andes, in part because of the numerous surface remains and rich burials but likewise because of its faithfully realistic art style. The modeled and painted pottery vessels reveal minute details of the world of the Mochica. The local flora and fauna are reproduced so accurately that the species can be identified. Sculptured head jars are so individual that they are properly called portraits. The vessels show the weapons and dress of the warriors, scenes of hunting and fishing, methods of punishment, types of diseases and their cure, house types, religious temples, ceremonies, dances, and, of course, a galaxy of mythological and supreme beings. Such a wealth of detail demands great self re-

41

Fig. 41. Stirrup-spout jar, with painted representation of warrior and jaguar. Mochica. Clay, 12″. Collection: Dr. Eduard Gaffron, courtesy The Art Institute of Chicago

straint on the part of the imaginative observer to refrain from over interpretation.

The pottery models of Mochica houses show rectangular floor plans, solid walls and pent or gabled roofs, in spite of the lack of direct rainfall in this area. However, the major Mochica architecture was directed towards the erection of great unit pyramids, some built on the open plains, others capping natural ridges. The effect is one of great mass with the high battered walls broken by terraces, platforms, and ramps. The pyramids were constructed almost entirely of rectangular, sun-baked adobe bricks, although rough stone might be used in the base foundation, and logs inserted as binders. The outer walls were coated with a clay plaster and painted in solid colors, or with figural designs, or cut out into relief clay arabesques.

The Huaca del Sol, not far from the town of Trujillo, is probably the largest of these pyramids. The base is a solid platform, 750 by 450 feet, and 60 feet high. A gross estimate of the number of bricks used in this structure runs over 130,000,000, clear evidence that the Mochica had a well organized labor force to execute this mammoth, but essentially unskilled, task.

The typical Mochica grave is a rectangular box tomb, lined and covered with adobe bricks. There is considerable variation in the quantity and quality of offerings placed in the graves, reflecting, no doubt, differences in the wealth and social status of the

Fig. 42. Stirrup-spout jar. Mochica. Clay, 10″ high. The painted design on this jar is a good example of the complexity of pattern sometimes found in Mochica painting. Collection: University Museum, Philadelphia. (39-20-53)

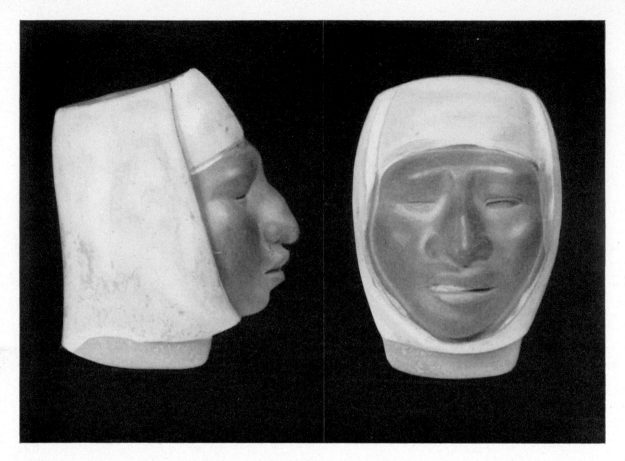

Fig. 43. Portrait jar. Mochica. Clay, 4⅛″ high. A fine example of realistic portraiture typical for this culture and otherwise very rare for pre-Columbian America. The solidity of sculptural form contrasts markedly with the delicacy of painted surface decoration shown in the preceding illustrations. Collection: Norbert Mayrock, Santiago, Chile

deceased. Preservation is not too good on the North Coast, due to the amount of saltpeter in the desert sands. Consequently, the more perishable artifacts of cloth, calabash, bone and wood are infrequently preserved. Nonetheless, from the few surviving textile fragments it is clear that this was an advanced craft. One pictorial vessel suggests that weaving was organized on a shop basis. At least, the scene shows a row of women with backstrap looms and a male supervisor sitting under a sun shade. Enough metal objects have been recovered to show skilled workmanship in gold and silver, and particularly in copper casting. There are also wooden boxes, idols, and staffs with copper points and realistically carved heads.

It is the ceramic art, however, which is preserved in greatest quantity and which is most representative of the Mochica. The better quality vessels were mold made. The outstanding characteristics of the Mochica ceramics are the skilled modeling and the delicate painting in red and cream white. The stirrup-spout vessel, although found in all North Coast periods, was a particular favorite of the Mochica. Other

Fig. 44. Jar in shape of a large draped head. (Spout has been broken off.) Mochica. Clay, $7\frac{1}{2}''$. Collection: University Museum, Philadelphia. (43370)

common vessel shapes are containers with cylindrical spouts and a curved, hollow handle; an outflaring flower vase; and a dipper-like bowl with a long conical side handle. However, in spite of the variety which detailed examination reveals, the Mochica ceramics as a whole present a consistent, uniform, and compact style. It is of interest to find a few vessels, clearly of Mochica manufacture, which depict the Chavín feline design, a persistent survival from the past.

Fig. 45. Jar in shape of a kneeling woman. (Here again the spout has been broken off.) Mochica. Clay, 6½″ high. Collection: University Museum, Philadelphia. (34282)

Fig. 46. Double vessel. Mochica. Clay, 6¾". If this vessel is dipped when filled with liquid, it emits a mournful sound, which accounts for the open mouth of the figure. Collection: Dr. Eduard Gaffron, courtesy The Art Institute of Chicago

The realistic designs, supplemented by other archeological information, give a broad picture of Mochica culture. The basic emphasis was on farming, as confirmed by the great attention to plants in the ceramic decoration, and by the remains of mammoth aqueducts which served as parts of the irrigation system. Hunting is depicted in the paintings as a sport for the privileged. There are scenes of beaters driving the animals into net enclosures where the special hunters wait with clubs and spears. The designs speak for the importance of marine life: clam, shrimp, lobster, and crab; fishing for ray, bonito, flying fish, and corbina.

The Mochica culture was certainly class divided although not as rigidly as Inca society. Nonetheless, the differential wealth in the burials and the numerous scenes

47

Fig. 47. Stirrup-spout jar, representing the mutilated head of a felon with feline heads on his headdress. Mochica. Hammered silver, 10½″ high. Collection: Peabody Museum, Harvard University. (52-30-30/7347)

which distinguish individuals of importance are sufficient to establish a class system. Likewise, there were many specialized groups, such as warriors, messengers, weavers, medicine men, priests, dancers, and musicians. The ceramic designs also indicate a hierarchy of gods represented by animals, birds, fish, plants, and humans, but further identification involves speculation.

In total, the Mochica pattern contained many of the elements which appear later in the Inca political empire. For example, the Mochica system seems to have been based on the manipulation of masses of unskilled laborers. Their expansion shows signs of a growing political organization and, at least, was effected by military conquest. Manufacturing and other forms of skilled activity were placed in the hands of specialized groups. The religion was not only based on a hierarchy of mythological beings, but was also organized and directed by a priest group. In spite of the high artistic achievements, there seems to have been an urge, later crystallized by the Inca, to reduce everything possible to unit labor and mass production.

Fig. 48. Figure painted with cinnabar. Mochica. Copper, 9″ high. Collection: Peabody Museum, Harvard University. (42-28-30/4334)

Above: Fig. 49. Stirrup-spout jar in the shape of a duck. Mochica. Clay, 8″ high. Collection: University Museum, Philadelphia. (29-190-3). *Left:* Fig. 50. Vessel. Mochica. Clay, 6½″ high. A rare example of the representation of a feline head in Mochica culture. Collection: University Museum, Philadelphia. (41-24-439)

PARACAS NECROPOLIS

The Paracas peninsula, near Pisco, was a burial ground for the Necropolis culture as well as for the Cavernas, previously described. The two cultures are certainly related and the major distinctions may reflect time since the two are assigned to different periods.

The Necropolis burials are found in subterranean, rectangular rooms, lined with rough stones and small adobes. In 1925, Julio C. Tello removed from these rooms over four hundred mummy bundles. They vary in size but a typical one, of conical shape, is about five feet in base diameter and five feet to the apex. The desiccated body occupies but a small portion of the bundle, the bulk being built up by numerous cloth wrappings. A description of one bundle will serve as a general illustration.

The body of the deceased had been viscerated and dried, and placed on a large circular shallow basket in flexed position, that is with the knees drawn up under the chin. Offerings had been put next to him, such as dried meat, wool, beans, maize, cotton, and peanuts. The body itself was dressed in simple clothing, and the head adorned with a turban to which feathers and gold ornaments were attached. Then layers of cloth had been wrapped around. At this point the upper portion of a plain cloth wrapping was bunched and tied to form a false head. The enlarged bundle with its false head was then treated as though it were the body. The false head was decorated with a turban, and the bundle adorned with shawls and shirts. The padding and wrapping process was continued and a new false head formed. In this bundle, there were four such stages of wrapping, which suggests a ceremonial procedure, perhaps at four different time periods, in which the bundle was dressed in new wrappings for the ceremony, and then reinterred. The outermost wrapping and some of the padding were of plain cloth, but many of the pieces were of the finest embroidery. There were a dozen sets of matched poncho shirts and shawls (see Fig. 55).

The Paracas Necropolis is justly famed for its turbans, ponchos, skirts, and shawls, characteristically decorated with over-all polychrome embroidery. The designs are elaborate stylized cat demons, birds, and anthropomorphized figures, arranged in repeat sequences, often alternating right side up and upside down. The accompanying ceramics are dull in contrast, with vessel shapes like those of Nazca to the south, but virtually devoid of decoration of any kind. Little is known about the Necropolis people except through their burials. They presumably lived in the neighboring valleys of Pisco, Ica, and Nazca but the sites are yet to be discovered. However, the embroidered designs are closely related to the Nazca polychrome ceramic painting.

The amount of time required to spin, dye, weave, and embroider any one of the thousands of large Paracas textiles must be estimated in years. Furthermore, the craft standards for the weaving were exceptionally high. In spite of the quantity of material, it is difficult to point to one piece which is better or poorer made than another, and the designs, in spite of their complexity, are amazingly consistent. Furthermore, as has been pointed out, many of the pieces were woven to the size of the enlarged bundle and were thus too large for practical use as clothing, nor do they show signs of wear that would result from daily use. The South Coast valleys are comparatively small, and could never have supported very large populations so that when quantity of

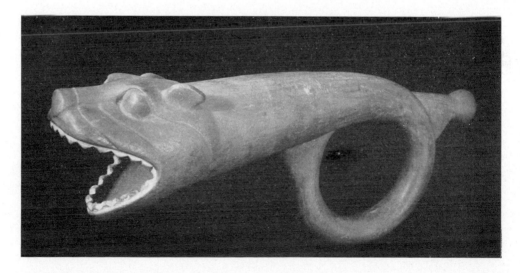

Fig. 51. Trumpet. Mochica. Clay, 16″ long. Collection: Peabody Museum, Harvard University. (46-77-30/5016)

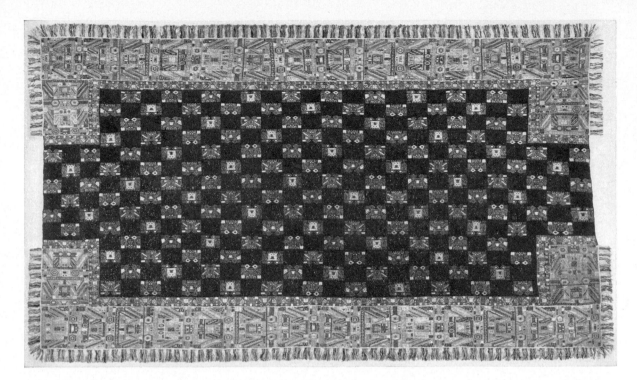

Fig. 52. Embroidered mantle. Paracas Necropolis. 93½″ long. The mantle shown above and the detail on the opposite page show the checkerboard pattern frequently found in Paracas textiles. This garment and those on the following pages were the result of careful design planning. It required several years to produce one of them. Collection: American Museum of Natural History, gift of Mrs. Kate Roberts Smith. (1953-22-1)

weaving is reviewed in terms of available weavers, we are presented with a picture of a people devoting the major part of their leisure time to the skilled production of textiles predestined to be interred with their ancestors. It is not surprising that such a people would be little concerned with the erection of great temples, or elaborate political systems, and as yet there is no archeological evidence for associated architecture nor implication of political advancement. Good organization will increase the production of ceramics and make possible the erection of mammoth pyramids, but there is no speed-up process in skilled, hand loom weaving except time and an increased number of weavers.

Fig. 53. Detail of embroidered mantle. Paracas Necropolis. American Museum of Natural History, New York. Photo Nickolas Muray

Fig. 54. Embroidered shirt, representative of the fabulous richness of ceremonial garments. Paracas Necropolis. 50″ high. Collection: American Museum of Natural History

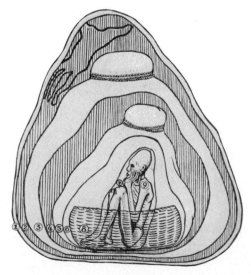

Fig. 55. Cross-section of a mummy bundle. The numbers apply to the wrapping of the mummy. Courtesy American Museum of Natural History

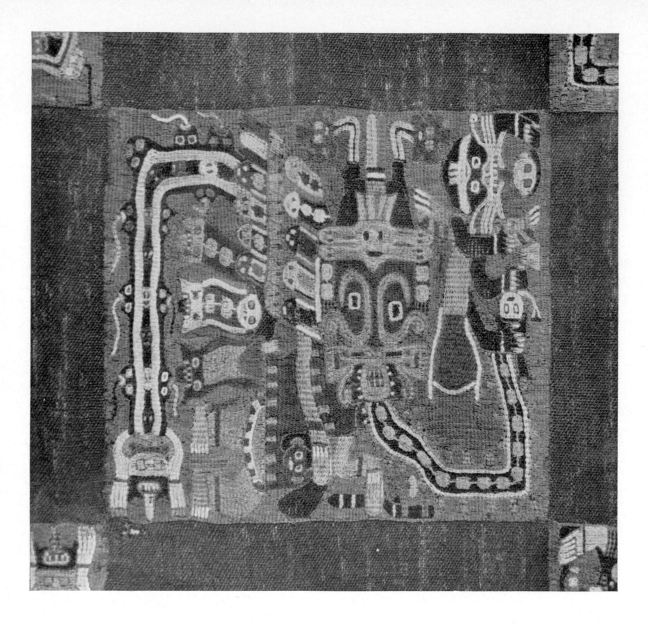

Fig. 56. Detail of mantle embroidered with jaguar design. Paracas Necropolis. Subject matter and style of this mantle resemble strongly the decoration used during the Nazca culture. Collection: Brooklyn Museum. (34.1557)

Fig. 57. Section of fabric made of knitted figures. Paracas Necropolis. This fabulous textile, which suggests a three-dimensional lace, is the only known complete example of this technique. Collection: Etnografiska Museet, Göteborg, Sweden. (35.32.179)

Fig. 58. Painted border of a mantle. Paracas Necropolis. 27″ long. An exceedingly rare example of the painting of that period. The design on this fabric is much freer and more alive than that found on the pottery and the weaving of Paracas Necropolis. Detail reproduced in color on the opposite page. Collection: The Cleveland Museum of Art, gift of Mrs. Henry Norweb. (40.530)

Fig. 59. Double-spout jar. Paracas Necropolis. Clay, 8″ diameter. A fine example of the simplicity prevalent in that style. The vessel is painted white, the tips of the spout are red. Collection: Peabody Museum, Harvard University. (46-77-30/5304)

Fig. 60. Detail of Paracas mantle reproduced on the opposite page. *Color plate courtesy the Cleveland Museum of Art*

Fig. 61. Embroidered mantle, with bold red figures on white background. Paracas Necropolis. 109″long. Collection: Peabody Museum, Harvard University. (32-30-30-45)

NAZCA

The Paracas Necropolis textile designs resemble those on the polychrome pottery of the Nazca culture, in the valleys of Nazca and Ica on the South Coast. There are, however, so many differences between the two cultures, that it cannot be argued that Necropolis was the burial ground for a Nazca population. Nazca, like Necropolis, emphasizes fine weaving and neglects architecture, although there are some buildings of ball and conical adobes. In the Necropolis weaving, over-all embroidery is characteristic and the same is true of Nazca although brocade, warp and weft stripe, gauze, and painted cloth are also prominent among the numerous weaving techniques practiced. Both cultures commonly use three-dimensional needle knitting to finish textile borders.

The Nazca graves are pot-shaped chambers entered through round or squared shafts. The graves contain cloth-wrapped burials, but these are not elaborate bundles, and also large quantities of ceramic vessels. The ceramics are distinguished by their shapes, designs, and polychrome colors. The most characteristic forms are bell-shaped cups, tall goblets, containers with two short tubular spouts connected with a flat bridge, and vessels with spout and bridge to modeled head. In general, Nazca modeling is neither very frequent nor too well executed. Instead, the ceramics are characterized by polychrome painting in as many as ten colors, including several shades of red, white, cream, grey, buff, black, yellow, brown, and violet. The designs on some of the early-phase vessels are simple, somewhat realistic representations of birds and animals. More typical, however, are the elaborate stylized designs of anthro-

Fig. 62. Bowl decorated with painted trophy heads. Nazca. Clay, 5⅜″ diameter. Collection: Dr. Eduard Gaffron, courtesy The Art Institute of Chicago

Fig. 63. Vase decorated with horizontal stripes. Nazca. Clay, 12¾″ high. Collection: Mr. and Mrs. René d'Harnoncourt, New York

Above left: Fig. 64. Bottle with handle in the shape of a person dressed in poncho and mantle. Nazca. Clay, 5¼″ high. Collection: Dr. Eduard Gaffron, courtesy The Art Institute of Chicago

Above right: Fig. 65. Beaker in the shape of a quail. Nazca. Clay, 8³⁄₁₆″ high. Collection: Dr. Eduard Gaffron, courtesy The Art Institute of Chicago

Right: Fig. 66. Bowl decorated with fisherman and nets. Nazca. Clay, 7¼″ high. Collection: Carlebach Gallery, New York

61

pomorphic monsters, felines with elongated bodies, and human figures carrying jagged staffs. In all of these, the basic figure is obscured by the addition of innumerable appendages.

Less is known about Nazca culture than Mochica partially because of fewer scientific excavations but also because the designs offer little aid for interpretation. Nazca is limited in distribution to the South Coast valleys and apparently lacked expansion tendencies. The impression is one of a people oriented toward religion, placing great emphasis on ancestor worship and burial.

On the deserts, flanking the Nazca valley, airplane pictures have revealed an intricate maze of lines that extend for miles and curve to form figures of various kinds. There has been much speculation about the purpose of these lines, or paths, all clearly of artificial construction. It is particularly provoking since the designs could only have been seen from the air. Some have suggested that they resulted from calendrical observations, or that they were symbolic representations of genealogical trees. They might also have been markers for ceremonial parades by a people who devoted much of their life to weaving for their ancestors and who thought nothing of marching for miles onto a desert peninsula to inter their dead.

Fig. 69. Bottle with handle. Nazca. Clay, 7³⁄₁₆″ high. The angular stylization of the fantastic animal used on this bottle reveals considerable Tiahuanaco influence. Collection: Dr. Eduard Gaffron, courtesy The Art Institute of Chicago

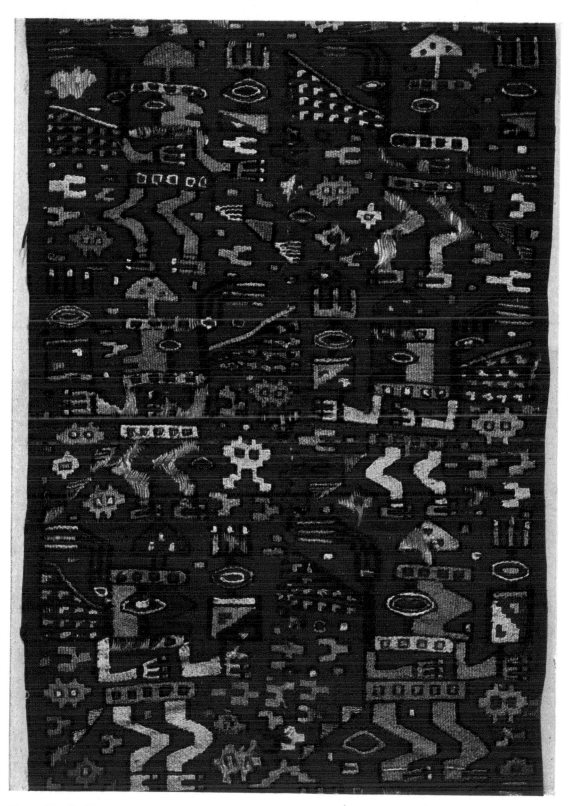

Fig. 70. Detail of fragment of Nazca fabric in tapestry weave with elaborate all-over pattern. 9⅞″ wide. Collection Nelson A. Rockefeller, New York. Photo Nickolas Muray

Fig. 71. Woven poncho. Nazca. 37″ long. Rare in its boldness and simplicity. Collection: The Cleveland Museum of Art, gift of Mrs. Henry Norweb. (40.514)

Fig. 72. Section of fabric in tapestry weave. Nazca. A good example of the tendency, in Nazca weaving, to dissolve images into symmetrical and geometric patterns. Collection: University Museum, Philadelphia. (SA 4734 a)

RECUAY

The Callejón de Huaylas basin is the upper branch of the Santa River which, unlike other coastal streams, runs parallel to the Pacific before it turns sharply and cuts through the western mountain range. This basin was the center of the Recuay culture, although it, like the river, spilled over to the adjacent coastal valleys. However, Recuay is known only through its highland manifestations and these are limited to those remains durable enough to withstand centuries of alternating rainy and dry seasons.

The Recuay houses and temples were constructed with large stone slabs, split and trimmed, but not dressed. Subterranean houses are particularly characteristic, some extending two or three stories below ground, but there are also surface constructions.

Stone carving is typical of Recuay and falls into two categories: slab lintels, decorated with high-relief felines represented with profile bodies and front-view faces; and seated figures carved in the round.

Recuay ceramics are noted for their great variety of shapes. Some of the common ones are open bowls with ring bases, conical-handled dippers, jars with large flat conical-handled disc-like rims, flat-topped vessels surmounted by groups of small modeled figures, and modeled jars representing humans, animals, warriors, and castles. Vessels are frequently made of a white kaolin clay, and painted in positive red and white or in more typical two- and three-color negative. The three-color negative is in reality only the standard resist black and white negative painting with the addition of positive red lines. Geometric design is most frequent but there are also figure representations of which the most outstanding is a jaguar with angular body and a projecting comb-like fret on the head.

Fig. 73. Llama vessel, with standing warrior. Recuay. Clay, 9⅜″ high. In Recuay pottery, elaborate surface pattern is combined with complex form, resulting in a somewhat chaotic total effect. However, details like the llama head are sensitive and charming. Collection: American Museum of Natural History. (B/8816)

Fig. 74. Jar decorated with negative painting. Recuay. Clay, 9½″ high. The stylized rendering of the animal with a small number of articulated lines is very ingenious, and unique in Peru. A somewhat similar treatment of animal form is found in faraway Coclé (see Fig. 185). Collection: American Museum of Natural History. (B/8272)

Although Recuay culture can be easily identified by its distinctive artifacts there is no clear-cut pattern which characterizes the whole. Instead, the sites, even in the Callejón de Huaylas, show local variation of sufficient magnitude to imply that there was no widespread religious or political organizations.

PERIOD FOUR (APPROXIMATELY 1000 TO 1300 A.D.)

The previous period was characterized by distinctive regional cultures, each the end product of a long sequence of technological development. Once techniques were perfected satisfactorily, the emphasis appears to shift to the development of political and social organization, together with expansionistic tendencies. The Mochica spread their culture and control to the north and the south. Artifacts characteristic of Recuay in the Callejón de Huaylas and of Cajamarca farther north now appear in the coastal valleys. In their last phase, even the peaceful Nazca people extended their influence over a wider area. That all of this expansion involved conflict was inevitable, and can be verified by detailed archeological studies. There is, for example, evidence of local population decline, and in some places irrigation systems apparently broke down since the cultivation reverts to the valley margins.

The fourth period is dominated by the Tiahuanaco culture which extended its influence and perhaps its control over most of the Central Andes. The Tiahuanaco expansion is traced by a distinctive design style, a ceramic type, a color scheme, and a weaving pattern. It is still uncertain whether the wide spread of these features was by peaceful or military means, but in any event, local cultures everywhere were either merged with Tiahuanaco or eclipsed. The major Tiahuanaco remains are found both in Bolivia and Peru, although the former country was probably the principal center.

BOLIVIAN TIAHUANACO

The famous ruins named Tiahuanaco lie on the Bolivian side of the Titicaca basin some twelve miles south of the lake. The *altiplano*, as this high structural basin is called, extends for several hundred miles between two mountain ranges but only the area close to Lake Titicaca is truly inhabitable. The lake, at 12,500 feet altitude, is the largest in the Andes, and a sufficient body of water to ameliorate the temperature, so that corn will grow on its shores. The lake contains some unique fish, the suchi and boga, which are still an important source of food for the Indian population. The lake region is picturesque but forbidding. Too high for trees, the bleak flats and hill slopes have a meagre cover of grass and brush. On every side are jagged, snow-capped peaks. Winds are constant and cold and violent storms not infrequent. Still the region supports a scattered but numerous Indian population today, and probably did much the same in the past.

The site of Tiahuanaco is certainly the most elaborate one, and the purest manifestation of the culture yet to be found. It is composed of a series of construction units spread out over an immense area. Although each unit is symmetrical within itself, no geometric system can be discovered in the over-all plan. The largest construction is a partially artificial, stepped pyramid, called Acapana, once stone faced. The ground plan is 690 feet square and the height, 50 feet. The flat top has house foundations and a large reservoir with a dressed-stone overflow. Acapana has every appearance of a fortified hill which could have served as a place of refuge in times of siege.

Northwest of this hill is a large rectangular unit, called Calasasaya, which measures

Fig. 75. Monolithic doorway ("Gate of the Sun") at Tiahuanaco, Bolivia. This site is believed to be one of the places of origin of the Tiahuanaco style, which spread widely throughout the highlands and coast of the Central Andean area. The lace-like pattern of the relief emphasizes the grandeur of the monolithic form. *Photo Pierre Verger*

some 445 by 425 feet, and is outlined with dressed-stone uprights. Because it looks today like an enclosure, it has often been misnamed a "stone henge." Actually, the enclosing rows of uprights are all that remain of the stone facing of a raised platform or terreplain. The typical Tiahuanaco facing technique employed stone uprights, set at intervals, and filled between with smaller blocks. These blocks have long since been removed and erosion plus years of plowing have lowered the old platform surface. The original platform construction once contained a sunken court with a megalithic stairway at its eastern end. The famous monolithic stone gateway, called the "Gate of the Sun," as well as several statues, are associated with this unit.

Several smaller ruins are found to the east and west of Calasasaya. In one of these, a small subterranean temple, was found the largest pillar-type statue of South America.

Some distance from the main group of ruins is the unit called Puma Puncu. It was constructed of massive sandstone and basalt blocks and slabs, some weighing over 100 tons, all carefully dressed and fitted together.

The Tiahuanaco site has suffered much destruction at the hands of more recent builders but even so there are indications that it had never been finally completed. In fact, Tiahuanaco, like Chavín de Huántar, was probably not a great population center, but was rather a religious site to which pilgrims came for annual ceremonies and were put to service hauling stones, dressing them, and constructing temple walls.

Tiahuanaco stone masonry is among the best in the Central Andes. Large and small sandstone or basalt blocks were carefully squared and polished, and fitted together by insets, tenons, notches, and even bound with copper cramps set into cut-out

Fig. 76. Detail of Fig. 75

Fig. 77. Sculptures. Tiahuanaco, Bolivia. Stone. These sculptures show a realism unusual in the Tiahuanaco style. *Photo Pierre Verger*

grooves. The facing technique of uprights and block fill is characteristic. The constructions emphasize mass, through raised platforms and pyramids. Stairways and monolithic gates form parts of the buildings and both statues and stone carving were used architecturally.

Many examples of stone carving have been found at Tiahuanaco. There are somewhat realistic statues representing kneeling or seated figures, with projecting cheek bones, jutting jaws, and flaring lips; boulder-like heads; pillars carved with simple features; and slabs with angular, geometric designs. Two other types of carving are particularly characteristic: namely, pillar-like statues covered with incised designs; and low-relief designs on flat surfaces.

The pillar-like statues pay less attention to the carving in the round than to the incised design detail (see page 16). They may be twenty or more feet high, and represent a standing figure with arms on the breast, one hand holding a goblet, the other clasping some object. The face is squared and surmounted by a decorated headband. The eyes are rounded squares with projecting tear bands below; the nose is in relief; the mouth an oval with squared teeth but no crossed fangs. The whole body is covered with fine incision, representing the textile designs on the garments portrayed.

The low-relief carving is found on lintels, monolithic gateways, and slabs. The most famous example is the low-relief frieze on the "Gate of the Sun" (Fig. 75), which serves as a résumé of Tiahuanaco style. In the center of the frieze is a front-view standing figure, in high relief, with each arm thrust out to the side, holding a staff adorned with puma and condor heads. The face is squared and surrounded by appendages which end in discs, puma heads, and condor heads. The figure wears shoulder straps and a

Fig. 78. Incense burner in the shape of a llama. Tiahuanaco, Bolivia. Clay, 19¼″ long. Like the stone figures on the preceding page, incense burners like this are among the few examples of realistic Tiahuanaco sculpture. Considering the formality of Tiahuanaco art, it is noteworthy that it can rise to such emotional intensity. Collection: American Museum of Natural History. (41.1/3848)

belt with appended tabs. On each side of this central figure are three rows of runners, each with bent knees and capes flowing behind. The runners of the central row wear condor masks. Along the base of the frieze is a row of front-view faces enclosed by a fretwork band. All of the designs represented in this frieze appear again and again in the pan-Peruvian spread of Tiahuanaco style, on ceramics, textiles, woodcarving, and other media.

Tiahuanaco vessels are confined largely to a few standard shapes, such as a flaring-sided goblet, a hollow-based libation bowl, modeled puma and llama vessels, vases, and squat open bowls with flaring sides. The ceramics are painted in polychrome colors which almost inevitably include black and white on an over-all red slip base. The typical designs are pumas, condors, human faces and figures, and geometric elements, generally outlined in black and filled in with various colors. It is interesting that the ceramic designs are basically different than those incised on the stonework, although they do overlap in details. At the same time, the incised stonework designs seem closely related to textile patterns. In the expansion of Tiahuanaco, it is the stonework-textile series of designs which spread.

Other Tiahuanaco ruins have been found in Bolivia but none of comparable elaboration. There is good evidence for the direct spread of Tiahuanaco influence from the Titicaca basin to eastern Bolivia and to northern Chile. However, the wider expansion which covered most of Peru presents a different problem.

Fig. 79. Head. Tiahuanaco, Bolivia. Stone, 2¼″ high. This small fragment, decorated with line engraving, retains much of the monumental quality of the Stela Bennett. Collection: American Museum of Natural History. (B/2787)

Fig. 80. Beaker. Highland Tiahuanaco. Clay, 6½″ high. A good example of the formality of the classic Tiahuanaco style expressed in painted decoration. Collection: University Museum, Philadelphia. (29-76-1)

Fig. 81. Fragment of a face. Coast Tiahuanaco. Clay, 3⅜″ high. Part of a large jar showing a realistic face covered with polychrome geometric designs. Collection: Dr. Eduard Gaffron, courtesy The Art Institute of Chicago

PERUVIAN TIAHUANACO

The Peruvian finds which can be assigned to the Tiahuanaco horizon share the following features: ceramics painted in black, white, and other colors on an over-all red base; the goblet and flaring-sided cup vessel shapes; fine tapestry with designs similar to those on the "Gate of the Sun"; and such specialized design elements as the puma, condor, trident, and step. Although this is an impressive list, it is clearly not the total Tiahuanaco pattern of the highland Bolivian center. Furthermore, everywhere in Peru the Tiahuanaco elements are mixed with the styles of the local cultures, as, for example, on the South Coast where the polychrome Tiahuanaco designs are found on vessels of Nazca shapes. In addition, Peruvian Tiahuanaco has some characteristic features, such as double-spout vessels, face-collar jars, and double bowls, none of which occurs in Bolivia.

Buildings of rough stone are found at Tiahuanaco sites in the Peruvian highlands but the characteristic dressed-stone masonry is lacking. At the site of Wari in the Mantaro basin there are also statues which resemble the Bolivian ones in form but lack the fine incised designs. On the coast, there are as yet no buildings which can be definitely assigned to the Tiahuanaco period, although many of the earlier constructions were re-used.

Fig. 82. Large vessel. Coast Tiahuanaco. Clay, 29″ high. Collection: American Museum of Natural History. (41.0/5314)

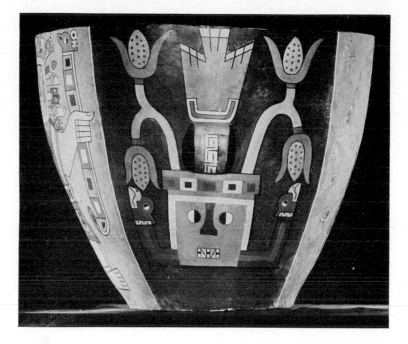

Coastal Tiahuanaco graves are noted for their textiles. Large cemeteries, like those of Ancón and Pachacamac on the Central Coast, contain sizeable mummy bundles with excellently woven wrappings. Brocade, double cloth, painted fabric, tie dye, and pile knot or velvet are all favorite techniques, but the polychrome tapestries are most characteristic. The tapestry designs almost always represent the same figures which adorn the stone statues and the frieze of the "Gate of the Sun" at the Tiahuanaco site in Bolivia. The ceramic designs are similar to those on the textiles, although freer in execution. The cemetery of Pacheco in the Nazca valley is particularly famed for its

Fig. 83. Bowl in the shape of a skull. Coast Tiahuanaco. Clay, 4¼″ high. Collection: American Museum of Natural History. (B/8222)

75

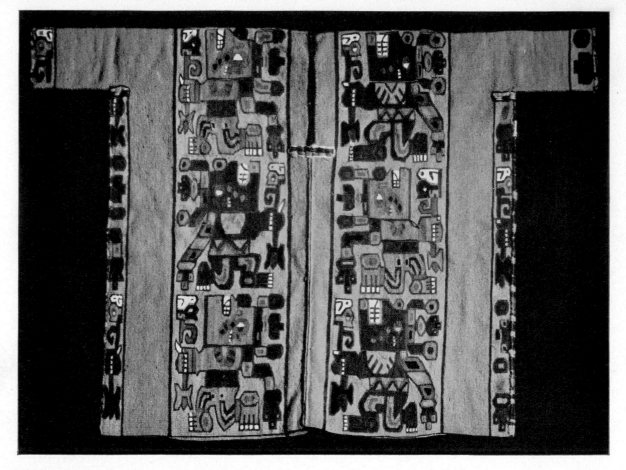

Fig. 84. Miniature shirt, back view. Coast Tiahuanaco. Tapestry weave, 12¼″ wide. Collection: Mr. and Mrs. A. B. Martin, courtesy The Brooklyn Museum. (L.48.13)

modeled llama vessels and thick U-shaped urns. The urns are decorated, inside and out, with a front-view figure identical in almost every detail with the central figure on the "Gate of the Sun." Other panels on these urns show designs of various plants, all of highland species (see Fig. 82).

The Peruvian and Bolivian manifestations of the Tiahuanaco culture are clearly related, although neither is directly derived from the other. The Peruvian ceramics share the polychrome colors and two major vessel shapes with Bolivia, but are otherwise distinct. The closest relationship is that of the Peruvian textile designs with those on Bolivian stone carving. Since the latter undoubtedly are intended to represent textile patterns it is quite possible that the wide spread of Tiahuanaco style came through the medium of textile distribution.

The Tiahuanaco expansion was certainly strongly motivated by organized religion. The Bolivian ruin has every appearance of a ceremonial center and the design of the frieze on the "Gate of the Sun" is the acme of religious symbolism. On the other hand,

Fig. 85. Detail of fragment of poncho in tapestry weave with highly stylized feline design. Coast Tiahuanaco. $19\frac{5}{8}''$ wide. Collection Nelson A. Rockefeller, New York. Photo Nickolas Muray

Fig. 86. Feather hat. Coast Tiahuanaco. 6¾″ high. A fine example of small feather mosaic. Collection: The Brooklyn Museum (41.228)

the spread created too great a disturbance of local cultures everywhere to have been merely strong religious influence, and consequently was probably accomplished by actual military invasion. The close uniformity of style throughout the whole area would imply that the movement was relatively rapid, but that it did not result in any long-time political unity is shown by its equally rapid breakdown. The expansion affected the local Peruvian cultures in different ways. On the South Coast, Tiahuanaco first merged with and then eliminated the Nazca culture which never reappears. The same thing happened to the Central Coast cultures. On the North Coast, however, there must have been stiffer resistance. Although the Mochica culture was temporarily eclipsed, it soon revived in somewhat modified form as the Chimu.

Fig. 87. Vessel. Coast Tiahuanaco. Clay, 12¼ high. The similarity in the treatment of subject matter between the design on this vessel and the design on the poncho illustrated on the opposite page shows that style occasionally becomes so important that it ignores the characteristics of specific techniques. Collection: Nelson A. Rockefeller

Opposite: Fig. 88. Section of poncho. Coast Tiahuanaco. Tapestry weave, 59¼" high. An excellent example of the transformation of representational art into a decorative all-over pattern. Collection: Robert Woods Bliss, courtesy The National Gallery of Art, Washington, D.C. (444)

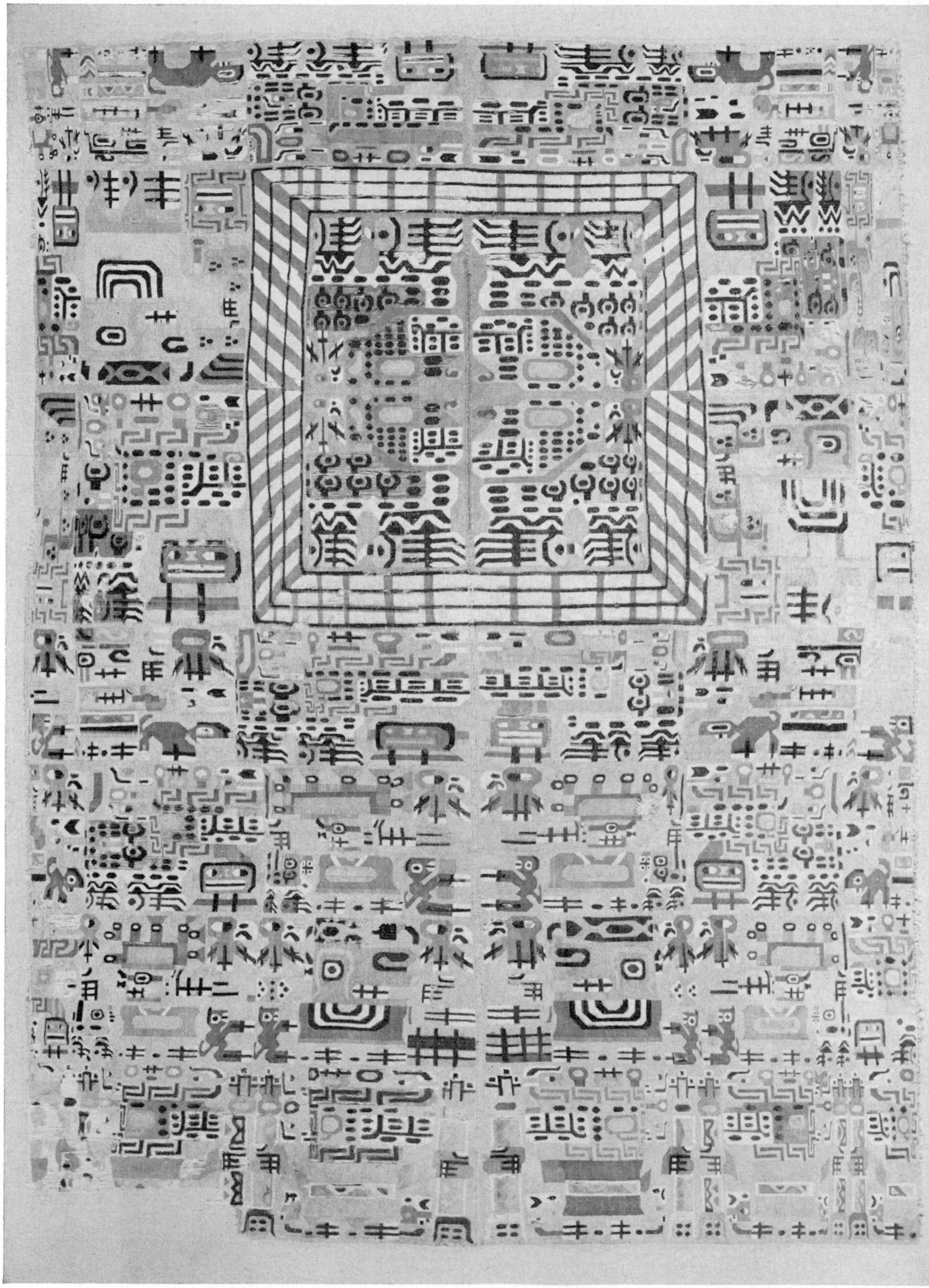

Fig. 89. Carved leeboard. Coast Tiahuanaco. Wood, 38″ high. This leeboard (detail reproduced in color on the opposite page) is a good example
of Tiahuanaco carving, which never violates the basic form of the object
to which it is applied. Collection: American Museum of Natural History,
gift of Mrs. Kate Roberts Smith. (1953-22)

Fig. 90. Detail of carved leeboard. Coast Tiahuanaco. Wood. American Museum of Natural History, New York. Photo Nickolas Muray

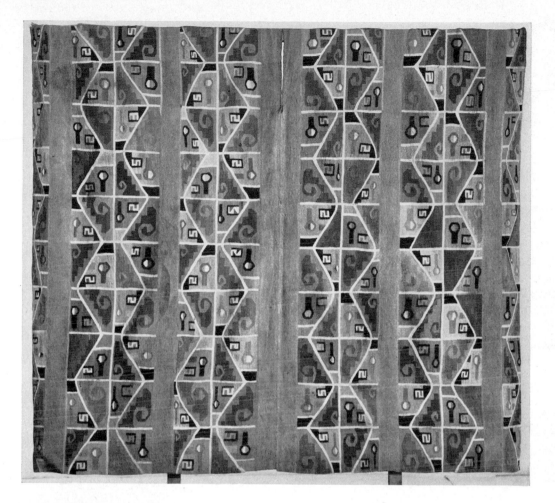

Above: Fig. 91. Poncho. Coast Tiahuanaco. Tapestry weave, c. 44"
long. An example of the most abstract rendering of the feline motif,
the rectangle with the S-shaped figure in it representing the mouth,
and the light disk in two colors the eye, of the feline. The spirals may
be the creature's tail. Collection: Dr. Eduard Gaffron, courtesy The
Art Institute of Chicago.

Left: Fig. 92. Painted textile fragment, showing the extreme freedom
of line. 15½" high. Coast Tiahuanaco. Collection: Mr. and Mrs.
René d'Harnoncourt

PERIOD FIVE (APPROXIMATELY 1300 TO 1438 A.D.)

Following the Tiahuanaco expansion, regional cultures re-emerge. Although the Tiahuanaco era had been disruptive, no techniques or skills were really lost and there were probably some new contributions. In any case, the new emphasis was now very definitely on political organization. As a result, populations were reshifted into large habitation centers, some of which reached city proportions. Because of the increased awareness of the threat of invasion, forts were built at strategic points and garrisons established at them. The shift in emphasis is reflected in the craft products which, although still produced competently and in quantity, lack quality and artistic inspiration. Most of the highland cultures of this period are nondescript, although buildings are numerous. The coastal cultures show more variety but no great distinction.

ICA

On the South Coast the late Ica culture continued the traditional interest in weaving but reduced the design units to small geometric elements, repeated over and over again. The same applies to the ceramics, which were painted in black, white, and red with over-all geometric designs copied directly from the textile patterns. On the other hand, building activity was intense and the many mechanically laid-out adobe constructions resemble public rather than religious centers.

Fig. 93. Jar. Ica. Clay, 14″ high. The small geometric patterns are characteristic of the style. Collection: American Museum of Natural History. (41. 1/3494)

Fig. 94. Large urn. Chancay. Clay, 15½" high. Most Chancay ceramics are decorated with simple geometric designs, but occasionally pieces like this are found that use representational subject matter in a lively manner. Collection: American Museum of Natural History. (X2.389)

Fig. 95. Vessel in the shape of a seated man. Chancay. Clay, 16″ high. In both form and design, Chancay ceramics are unlike those of the major Peruvian cultures. They seem closer to some of the work from the northern Andes and the Amazon basin. Collection: American Museum of Natural History. (B8365)

CHANCAY

The Central Coast valleys are dominated by the Chancay culture which was apparently well organized politically. The most typical ceramics are open bowls, flaring-rim jars and face-collar vessels, decorated in black on a flaky white slip with crudely executed geometric designs of perpendicular and wavy lines, crosshatch, checkers, and other such simple units. Less common are examples with representational subject matter.

CHIMU

The Mochica culture on the North Coast was not, as previously pointed out, totally eliminated by the Tiahuanaco expansion. Instead, the Chimu culture represents a partial re-emergence of Mochica, modified by Tiahuanaco influence, and embellished with some new innovations, largely in the sphere of political organization. The Chimu control was extensive, including the two rich northern valleys of Lambayeque and Piura, and those to the south as far as Casma. The population was large and well organized. Extensive irrigation systems allowed the cultivation of every available acre of land. The Chimu are noted for their large city units of two types: the garrison town located at strategic defense spots; and the ceremonial cities.

Chanchan, near Trujillo, is one of the largest ceremonial cities. In total, it covers over eight square miles and contains ten major units. Within each enclosure are pyramids, rows of houses, stone-walled reservoirs, irrigated gardens, and cemeteries. The building is almost entirely of large rectangular adobes, and the walls are coated with clay plaster and often decorated with relief arabesques of rows of birds, humans, and animals. The tops of the walls may be capped with adobe bricks arranged to form diamond or fret patterns.

The Chimu ceramics are predominately of smoked blackware. There are also redware vessels, and rarely a positive-painted piece. The stirrup-spout container is still a favorite, reflecting the earlier Mochica, but there are new shapes introduced by the

Fig. 96. Stirrup-spout jar. Chimu. Clay, 9½″ high. This is a typical piece of Chimu blackware decorated with a pressed design. The fantastic creatures frequently found on these vessels are reminiscent of surrealist imagery. Collection: Peabody Museum, Harvard University. (75577)

Above: Fig. 97. Cup with puma and cubs. Chimu. Silver, 4″ high. Collection: Charles Lucien Morley, New York

Left: Fig. 98. Stirrup-spout vessel, in the form of a puma nursing cubs. Chimu. Clay, 9⅞″ high. The likeness between these two beautifully executed pieces is so striking that one wonders if this particular style originated in hammered silver or in modeled clay. Collection: Dr. Eduard Gaffron, courtesy The Art Institute of Chicago

Tiahuanaco culture, such as double whistling jars, double spouts, and spout-and-bridge vessels, and a great variety of cooking ollas. Ceramics are still mold made and decorated by relief and modeling. The designs and sculptured figures still represent birds, animals, and scenes of various kinds but the art lacks the realism and the quality of the Mochica predecessors.

The Chimu weavers produced great quantities of textiles and although these are not exceptional in their designs, the double cloth, outline embroidery, and tapestries are of excellent quality. Feather mosaic pieces are particularly outstanding. The Chimu were also excellent metallurgists. Copper was extensively used for knives, club heads, axes, and points for digging sticks. Gold and silver were employed for goblets with relief designs, breast plates, plumed helmets, and delicately incised ear cylinders ending in ornamented discs.

The early Spanish documents contain a few rare accounts of the "Kingdom of Chimor," as the Chimu organization was called. It is described as a sharply class-divided society with a definite ruling group and great masses of commoners. Once again most of the features which characterize the Inca Empire are already present in the Chimu pattern.

Fig. 99. Stirrup-spout vessel in the form of an embracing couple. Chimu. Clay, 7 15/16″ high. A fine example of fluid form in Chimu blackware. Collection: Dr. Eduard Gaffron, courtesy The Art Institute of Chicago

Fig. 100. Beaker in form of a head. Chimu. Gold, 6⅝" high. A very fine
example of a type frequently found in both gold and silver. Collection: Dr.
Eduard Gaffron, courtesy The Art Institute of Chicago

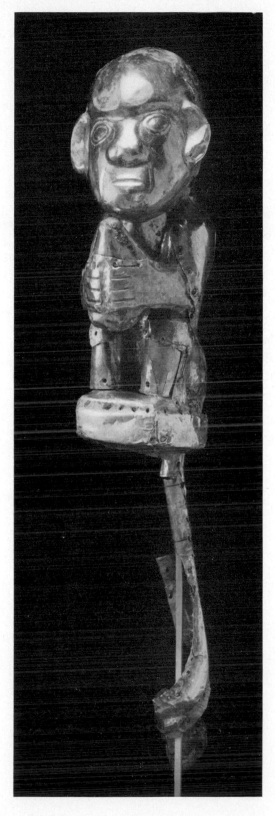

Fig. 101. Figure of a monkey. Chimu. Gold, c. 14½″ high. Probably the finial of a cane, as indicated by the tail that seems to have curled around a slender staff. Collection: The Cleveland Museum of Art, James Albert Ford Memorial Collection. (49.197)

Fig. 102. Beaker covered with very elaborate repoussé design. Chimu. Silver, 9½" high.
Collection: Heeramaneck Galleries, New York

Above: Fig. 103. Earspools. Chimu. Gold, 3½″ wide. Very graceful and playful design, executed with great attention to detail. Collection: Nelson A. Rockefeller

Right: Fig. 104. Ceremonial axe. Chimu. Gold with turquoise and shell inlay, c. 17″ high. An example of the sumptuousness of Chimu ritual objects. Collection: Museo Nacional de Arqueología y Antropología, Peru

Fig. 105. Mask from mummy bundle, with wig and wrappings in place. Chimu. Wood, 9½″ high. Collection: American Museum of Natural History. (B/628)

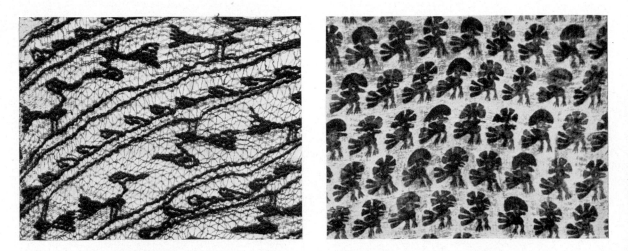

Left: Fig. 106. Section of veiling with bird design. Chimu. Collection: Brooklyn Museum. (29.1424-B). *Right:* Fig. 107. Detail of a large gauze hanging stamped with a bird pattern. Chimu. Size of entire piece: 117″ x 132″. Private collection, Museum für Völkerkunde, Munich

PERIOD SIX (APPROXIMATELY 1438 TO 1532 A.D.)

The final period brings us to the Inca whose achievements and empire organization are next described. The review of the early history has shown that most of the features of Inca culture were based on past cultural developments. So far as is known, the Inca had long been a loosely organized group in the Cuzco basin. The earlier archeological remains do not indicate that this region was one of any outstanding distinction. The Cuzco basin is, however, more isolated than any other, so that the Inca probably had many relatively undisturbed years in which to perfect their organization.

THE INCA EMPIRE

In 1532 when Francisco Pizarro sailed from Panama down the Pacific coast to Peru, he encountered and eventually destroyed the Inca Empire, the only truly organized political state of the New World in pre-Columbian times. It was not by accident that Pizarro found this Empire since its fame had spread to Panama and through the plains of Argentina to the mouth of the Plata River. So widespread in fact was the fame of this fabulous empire, that the Spaniards first attempted to reach it by the back door, as it were, via Paraguay and Argentina. It is said, for example, that metal scissors given to Indians at the mouth of the Amazon reached the Peruvian highlands before the Spaniards arrived there, and it is known that gold objects made in Peru are found in pre-Columbian graves in Panama.

The Empire was large in size. At the maximum, it included the mountain and coastal area from the southern border of Colombia to central Chile, a total of some 350,000 square miles, the equivalent of the Atlantic seaboard states of the United States. There is considerable disagreement about the population figures for the Empire, but an estimate of seven million does not seem excessive either in terms of the early accounts, the archeological remains, or the contemporary population figures for the same terrain.

This vast territory with its divergent populations was welded into a true political state founded on organized military conquest. The Inca were not content merely to extract tribute from the conquered people but instead tried to incorporate them into a political whole. Once a people was subdued, the process of incorporation was systematically applied. A topographic model of the region was made and a census taken. Forts were built and army garrisons established. Roads were constructed to link the new territory into the system. Important hostages and the most sacred of the local religious objects were taken to the Inca capital of Cuzco. If the population continued rebellious, whole villages might be moved out to another section and pacified groups moved in to replace them. In many cases the local rulers were left in command of the region, provided that their allegiances were shifted to the Inca overlord.

The Inca Empire was based on intensive agriculture. Over forty domesticated plants were cultivated, many of them well-known American species such as corn, bean, squash, potato, cotton, and tobacco; others less well-known, but adapted to high altitude farming, such as quinoa, oca, olluco, and mashua, all still grown by the native

93

population of the Andes today. The agricultural activities were supplemented by herding of the domesticated llamas and alpacas. Fishing was important along the coast and in some of the lakes, but hunting was reserved for the Inca as a privilege sport. Although here described as part of the Inca pattern, it is worth noting that all of these domesticated plants and animals, as well as the agricultural techniques, had long been established in the Central Andes.

The Inca technology was advanced, especially in ceramics, metallurgy, weaving, and architecture, but here again the various techniques and skills were part of the heritage from the past, since, with the possible exception of the alloy of copper and tin to form bronze, no specific technological innovations can be attributed to the Inca themselves. Instead, the great genius of the Inca, which allowed them to build and maintain an empire, was in organization. The political system, and in turn the economic, can be described as a basically decimal pyramidal pattern. At the base of the pyramid was the *puric*, an able-bodied male worker. Ten workers were controlled by a straw boss; ten straw bosses had a foreman; ten foremen in turn had a supervisor, ideally the head of a village. The hierarchy continued in this fashion to the chief of a tribe, reportedly composed of ten thousand workers, to the governor of a province, to the ruler of one of the four quarters of the Inca empire, and finally to the emperor, the Sapa Inca, at the apex of the pyramid. In the functioning of the system, reports flowed up, orders flowed down, but there was very little communication between officers of the same rank. This has often been claimed as one of the great weaknesses of the system since when Pizarro seized the emperor himself there was no one authorized to give the orders.

It is quite clear from the concepts on which the political organization was based that the Inca Empire was sharply class divided. The aristocratic class was composed

Fig. 108. Vessel. Inca. Stone, 26¼″ long. A large ceremonial vessel decorated with snakes in high relief. Collection: University Museum, Philadelphia. (SA 4681)

Fig. 109. Vessel in shape of a llama head. Inca. Stone, 4⅝″ high to rim. Collection: Chicago Museum of Natural History. (3314)

basically of the Inca and the royal family but also included, at a slightly lower level, the rulers of conquered areas and their families. The great mass of the population, however, formed the commoner class which supported the system. The distinctions between the aristocracy and the commoners were marked. All the higher political positions were reserved for the aristocracy. They wore finer clothing, had more solidly constructed houses, enjoyed the exclusive rights to fine ornaments, and had many other special privileges. Education, beyond the practical, was reserved for the upper classes. This duality affected the total system. In every topic of discussion, the distinction must be made between the aristocracy and the commoners. Virtually all of the descriptions of the glory that was the Inca Empire refer to the aristocratic class. The commoners, on the other hand, led a relatively drab and colorless life with little or no chance of escaping from their position.

In a system which emphasized efficient organization, specialists were numerous. Some, like the architects, military leaders, priests, and teachers, were drawn from the aristocracy; others, like the specialized weavers and metal workers, were selected from the commoners and supported by the state. However, many of the impressive achievements which characterize the Inca, such as the elaborate network of roads, the intricate irrigation systems, and the massive buildings, really required only a few specialists and depended largely on an organizational pattern which reduced the construction job to the level of unskilled laborers.

The dualism within the Inca system is well illustrated by religious practices. The Inca state religion, superimposed on all sections of the Empire, was complex and marked by elaborate ceremonies. In contrast, the religious practices in the local villages of the commoners consisted of simple rituals for curing the fields and the sick.

The basic concepts behind the state religion and the home practices were somewhat

Fig. 110. Large urn resembling the Greek aryballos. Inca. Clay, 44″ high. Inca ceramics were made in only a few shapes, distinctive for their dignity and beauty of proportion. Most decorations were geometric, and such representations as shown in the plates on the opposite page are rare and may well go back to Nazca influence. Collection: University Museum, Philadelphia. (SA 4615)

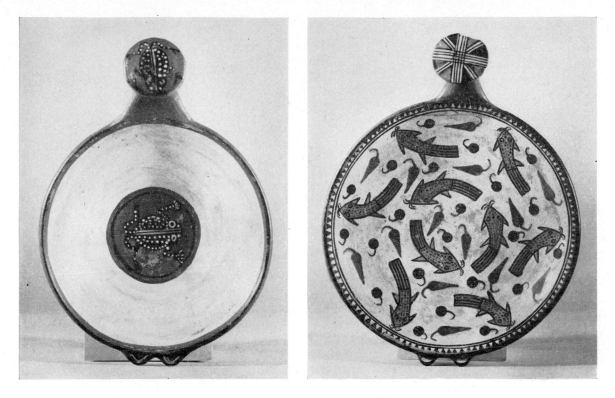

Left: Fig. 111. Shallow dish with turned-up handle; toad design in center and on handle. Inca. Clay, 7 9/16″ diameter. Collection: Dr. Eduard Gaffron, courtesy The Art Insitute of Chicago. *Right:* Fig. 112. Shallow dish with turned-up handle; fish pattern on white ground. Inca. Clay, 9 3/8″ diameter, Collection: Dr. Eduard Gaffron, courtesy The Art Institute of Chicago

similar. Ceremonies, both simple and complex, generally followed the agricultural cycle. The cult of the dead was prominently reflected in the burial practices, in ancestor worship, and by considerable concern about ghosts. Nature worship was also one of the dominant themes. The concept of *huaca*, special spiritual power, was attributed to all sacred places. The word *huaca* is still used today in reference to any ancient remains, in particular to burial grounds.

There is no question of the powerful grasp of religion on the people. Enormous amounts of time were devoted to the preparation of materials, the performance of ceremonies, and the support of the state religion. The major state ceremonies of the year were exceptionally elaborate affairs, directed in part towards impressing the public.

The early documents offer rich details on many aspects of the Inca culture, and the numerous archeological remains serve to confirm the historical records. Although the conquering Spaniards shipped many examples of Inca craftsmanship back to Spain, few if any of these collections have been preserved. Consequently, the principal collections of Inca artifacts are the results of relatively recent archeological investigations.

Inca ceramics are particularly distinctive and easy to identify. The vessel shapes

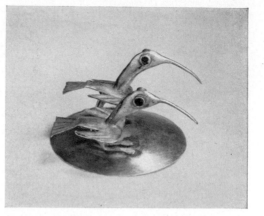

Fig. 114. Alpaca. Inca. Silver, 9⁷⁄₁₆" high. Collection: American Museum of Natural History.
(B 1619)

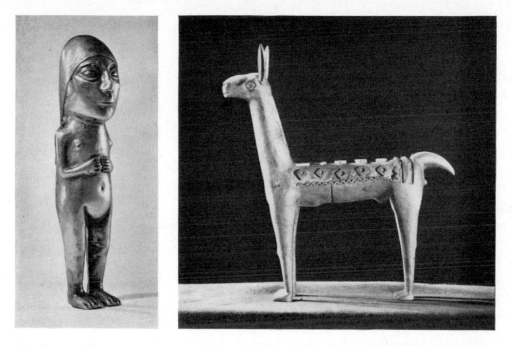

Left: Fig. 115. Figure of a woman. Inca. Silver, 6⅛″ high. Collection: American Museum of Natural History. (B/9608). *Right:* Fig. 116. Llama. Inca. Silver with gold appliqué, 9⅛″ high. Collection: American Museum of Natural History. (B/1618)

are highly standardized. The aryballos shape is perhaps the most characteristic, with conical base, vertical side handles, tall neck with flaring rim, and animal-head nubbin on the shoulder. Other typical shapes are a shallow dish with single, bird head, handle; a pedestal beaker, sometimes with a cover; and a single- or double-handled pitcher or bottle. The designs are generally polychrome, painted in bright colors of black, white, red, yellow, and orange. Most designs are geometric combinations of bands, diamonds, squares, checkers, triangles, crosshatch, circles, and dots, but there are also representations of butterflies, bees, animals, and block-like humans.

Much of the Inca weaving was for clothing, and the standard costume included breech clouts, wrap-around skirts, shawls, slit-neck ponchos, waist bands, head bands, and carrying bag with shoulder straps. Blankets and wall hangings were also woven, and great quantities of cloth were required for mummy wrappings. The weaving de-designs are largely geometric. Particularly characteristic are slit-neck poncho shirts in tapestry decorated with innumerable small geometric elements.

Mining was one of the standard tax obligations of the commoners, and the copper, tin, gold, and silver obtained from mines or washed from the river gravels were turned over to specialists trained as metallurgists. Both copper and bronze were cast and hammered into sharp points for digging sticks, star-shaped club heads, knives with curved blades, axes, chisels, needles, and pins. Gold and silver were used for the ornaments of the aristocracy. The early Spanish were greatly impressed by the amount of gold and silver work in the common possession of the Inca: walls and thrones are described as covered with gold; the emperor dined on gold and silver service; his gardens contained delicate butterflies and beds of flowers, all of cast gold. The contemporary collections verify these stories in part. They contain gold plates and silver goblets with hammered relief, cast silver llamas, and silver figurines with inlaid gold bands.

For the most part the Inca neglected stone sculpture and decorative carving but made many small objects of stone. The most characteristic are the stellate clubheads, small carved llamas with a hole in the back, presumably for offerings, and beautifully polished stone bowls, some with relief designs. Wood was also employed for many tools. Outstanding are the wooden goblets, called *kerus*, with lacquered designs. The lacquer technique was probably a Spanish introduction and the designs on the *kerus* often show individuals in European garb, but both plain and incised goblets occur earlier.

The Inca are famed for the quantity and variety of their stone constructions. They are particularly noteworthy as road builders since their elaborate system of highways formed a network throughout the entire Empire. Other types of construction work include irrigation systems, agricultural terraces, public buildings, temples, forts, and villages. In the highlands most of the building was done with stone, either split or carefully dressed, but on the coast the Inca followed the customs of their predecessors and built with sun-baked adobe brick.

Inca highland stone masonry presents several different styles, all contemporaneous, but used in terms of the function of the wall being built. One style utilizes unit-size blocks, carefully dressed on all four sides or, as a variant, left slightly rounded on the outer face. Another style, described as polygonal, employs blocks of different shapes and sizes, each carefully fitted with the adjacent ones. In the fortress of Sacsayhuaman, above Cuzco the walls are built with immense blocks weighing many tons, but the polygonal style is also represented by walls in Cuzco with much smaller blocks. It is obvious that the dressing and fitting of these irregularly shaped blocks must have been done at the site of construction itself, with each stone being carefully ground down until it would fit precisely with its neighbors.

The amount of such construction work is almost unbelievable. Modern Cuzco still reveals many well preserved walls of the Inca capital, and the last earthquake uncovered numerous other Inca walls which successfully withstood this earthquake as they had those of the past. Near Cuzco are many other sites of Inca construction. One of the best known is the city of Machu Picchu which covers a high sharp ridge above the Urubamba river with rooms, terraces, and temple units. Although the Cuzco district has the greatest concentration of these buildings, typical dressed and rough stone Inca walls are found to the north as far as Quito, Ecuador, and south to Bolivia and Argentina.

The Inca expansion was the most extensive ever witnessed in the Andean region. Although the Tiahuanaco influence extended into eastern Bolivia and northern Chile

Fig. 117. Large beaker (*keru*). Inca. Wood, with teeth, eyes, and spots of leopard inlaid in bone and gold, 9⅝" high. Collection: Mr. and Mrs. René d'Harnoncourt, New York

Fig. 118. Poncho; black and white checkerboard pattern with red top. Inca. Wool, 37½" high. Collection: Museum für Völkerkunde, Munich

Fig. 119. Veiling dyed in many colors. Inca. Wool, 74" x 38". Collection: Museum für Völkerkunde, Munich

Fig. 120. Cloak with puma and bird design. Inca. Feathers, 31″ high. Collection: Dr. Eduard Gaffron, courtesy The Art Institute of Chicago

Fig. 121. Walls of temple in Machu Picchu, showing the heroic setting of the city. Inca. Stone. The beauty of Inca stone architecture rests entirely on its exquisite stonework and the basic form of the building. In spite of the Inca's proven ability as sculptors (see Fig. 109), sculptured decorations are completely missing in their architecture. *Pierre Verger*

Fig. 122. Wall with three windows, Machu Picchu. Inca. *Photo Heinrich Ubbelohde Doering*

Fig. 123. Sacred cave, Kenco. The carved seats and the carving on walls and ceiling make this cave a sculpture in space.
Photo Heinrich Ubbelohde Doering

Fig. 124. Stairway, entrance to ceremonial cave, Machu Picchu. *Photo Pierre Verger*

in general the earlier cultural unity was limited to the Central Andes, and the mountainous regions to the north and south of this had quite independent cultural developments. This again does not mean that they were totally isolated and, in fact, many of the Central Andean traits and techniques have a pan-Andean distribution. However, the archeologist who works first in Peru and then in Colombia realizes that he is in a different world in spite of the standard ceramics, metal work, and textiles. On the other hand, if he works first on the North Coast of Peru and then in the Titicaca basin he still feels at home.

Fig. 125. Great Wall, Ollantaytambo. The blocks constituting this wall are all over ten feet high, and four to five feet wide. They are made of pale pink granite to contrast with the grey stone of the local rock which was used for all other constructions. The pink granite blocks had to be brought across a mountain and a river, involving fabulous labor. Their selection can be assigned only to ceremonial or esthetic reasons. *Photo Heinrich Ubbelohde Doering*

Fig. 126. Section of wall, Ollantaytambo, showing the unbelievably fine quality of stonework, which enabled the Incas to achieve perfect fit between two blocks, even where contours were not in straight lines. It is actually impossible to slip a knife between these stones. *Photo Heinrich Ubbelohde Doering*

Fig. 127. Stone wall, Sacsayhuaman. The stone on the extreme right is over twenty feet high. *Photo Pierre Verger*

TECHNIQUES OF THE CENTRAL ANDES

Archeological remains are exceptionally plentiful and varied in the Central Andes. Surface ruins are innumerable both in the highlands and on the coast, and range from simple isolated habitation sites to elaborate pyramids, ceremonial centers, and enormous cities. The rubbish heaps and the cemeteries yield a great variety of ceramics, metal objects, textiles, basketry, reed, shell, bone, stone, calabash, and woodwork. The greatest variety is found on the coast due to the remarkable preservation of objects found in the desert sands. In the rainy highlands only the more durable objects have escaped destruction.

Most of the archeological remains can best be described in terms of specific regions and periods. However, for three of the major crafts, ceramics, metallurgy, and weaving, some brief notes on common techniques seem appropriate. Most of these techniques were long known and practiced in the Central Andes, although at particular times and places certain ones were preferred.

CERAMICS

Clays suitable for pottery are found everywhere in the Central Andes although with some variation in quality. Some of the clays can be used directly by the potter but for most a temper must be added, such as mica for the highland clays to make them more plastic, and ground-up sand, shell, or potsherds for the coastal clays to make them less plastic.

The clay was shaped by several different methods. The simplest method was to hand mold the lump of clay into the desired shape, but the commonest was the coil method in which long cylinders, formed by rolling the clay between the hands, were coiled in rows to build up the walls of the vessel. The coil marks were rarely left visible but instead were carefully smoothed off with damp cloths, scrapers, and stone polishers. A third method, called paddle and anvil, was used both for original shaping and for finishing vessels. In this, a smooth stone is placed on the inner wall of the vessel and the outside is pounded with a flat wooden paddle. Still a fourth method, most commonly employed on the north coast of Peru, utilized a mold. Although clay molds have been found, not too much is known about the exact way in which they were used. In any case, the use of molds did not lead to great duplication of vessel shapes. Although the potter's wheel was unknown in ancient Peru, a somewhat similar effect was gained by placing the clay on a broken potsherd which could then be whirled around by hand.

The vessels were fired, sometimes to extreme hardness, either in open fires, pit ovens, or perhaps in kilns. In one method of firing the amount of oxygen was definitely reduced, resulting in a dark-colored or black clay. In another, the oxygen was increased by the use of a forced draft which produced a light-color clay. Some vessels were deliberately smoked black, like bucchero ware.

Most vessels, except some of the common cooking pots, were decorated before firing, and each culture had its favorite form of surface decoration. Common ones

Fig. 128. Plaque. Coast Tiahuanaco. Gold, 17″ x 18″. This is one of a set of many hammered gold plaques with repoussé design which may have been used as wall coverings. Collection: Museo Nacional de Arqueología y Antropología, Peru

are incision, with sharp or grooved lines; punch mark, with reed or dull implements, stamping with carved relief stamps pressed into the soft clay; appliqué, in which pellets or strips of clay are applied to the surface; and painting with from one to ten colors. Painted vessels were usually first covered with a thin over-all clay wash, called a slip, on which the design colors were applied. Negative painting was also used, in which the design areas were first covered with some resist material, such as wax or more likely strips of clay, and then the whole vessel was dipped in the dye or paint. When the resist strips were removed, the design was left in the base color, surrounded by black. Modeling was a favorite decorative device, either by shaping the whole vessel, or by adding modeled lugs to various parts of the pot. Relief decoration was achieved with carved stamps or molds.

Vessel shapes vary with each culture and period, although some, like globular cooking pots and open bowls or dishes, are found everywhere. Some common forms are stirrup-spouts, in which two arched tubes meet to form a single spout; double-spout jars, with two tubular spouts connected by a flat bridge; spout and bridge to modeled head or figure; double jars in which two containers are joined with tube and bridge; goblets; pitchers; cups; and many others.

METALLURGY

Metals were extensively used for making tools and ornaments throughout the Andes. Gold, silver, and copper were the commonest metals, although some use was also made of tin and mercury, and, very rarely, lead and platinum. The metals were obtained in open or pit mines and washed from mountain streams. Although some were found in a more or less pure form, others had to be refined. The metals were smelted in clay furnaces, a forced draft being provided by blowing through tubes or by locating the furnaces in spots where the prevailing winds could be so utilized. Some metals were used alone but intentional alloys were also common. Gold was mixed with silver and with copper, or with both, to form the alloy known as *tumbaga*. In the Inca period, at least, the bronze alloy of copper and tin was common.

Gold was cold-hammered into sheets which could then be cut out into shapes, or embossed, probably with a bone tool on a leather anvil, or designed in repoussé by hammering over carved molds. Several methods were employed to join pieces of metal. The simplest ones were by clinching, that is by folding and fitting the edges of the two pieces together, and by welding, which involves heating and hammering. Soldering was achieved by mixing a copper salt powder with a gum and applying this to the surfaces to be joined. The application of heat reduced the copper salts to metallic form and fused the edges.

Casting was well developed. Rough casts were made in open molds and the pieces later reshaped by heating and hammering. Hollow casting was done by the *cire perdue* method. In this, a core of fine clay mixed with charcoal is carved into shape, coated with wax, and placed in an outer clay mold with vents so arranged that the hot metal poured in replaces the wax. The core can later be powdered and removed. There were two techniques of gilding: one by coating the piece with a mixture of mercury and powdered gold so that heat would drive off the mercury and deposit the gold; the other by lining a mold with gold leaf before hot copper was poured in. The coloring technique called *mise en couleur* was used on alloys of copper and gold to imitate gild-

Fig. 129. Knife with inlaid handle, shaped into a llama head. Southern Highlands. Bronze, 6¼" high. Adze in the form of a bird. Southern Highlands. Bronze inlaid with copper and silver, 3½" high. Excellent examples of cast metal work from Peru. Collection: Robert Woods Bliss, courtesy The National Gallery of Art, Washington, D.C.

Fig. 130. Ceremonial hat. Coast Tiahuanaco. Velvet, c. 5¼″ high. Collection: The Cleveland Museum of Art, the J. H. Wade Fund. (45.378)

ing. Application of an acid to the alloy eats away the copper and floats the gold.

WEAVING

Weaving was the outstanding craft of ancient Peru. Although the textiles are best preserved on the dry coast, there is indirect evidence, and even an occasional find, to show that weaving was practiced in the highlands as well. The quantity of weaving indicated by the recovered fragments is almost unbelievable and goes far beyond any imaginable strictly utilitarian needs. Indeed, some of the coastal mummy bundles are wrapped with elaborately decorated textiles apparently woven for the sole purpose of interment. The ancient Peruvian weavers practiced every technique known to hand-loom weavers in the world and some unknown anywhere outside Peru. Furthermore, most of these techniques can be shown to appear early in the archeological sequence.

The domesticated cotton and the wool from the llamas and alpacas were the basic fibers, although there was some use of bast fibers and occasionally human hair. The cottons presented as many as six natural colors and the wool provided several shades of brown as well as black and white. However, both vegetable and mineral dyes were extensively used particularly for the wools, and as many as 190 hues have been distinguished.

The fibers were spun on slender spindle shafts essentially by hand twisting, although the drop-spindle method may also have been used. The resulting threads are of amazing fineness by modern measure. For example, M. D. C. Crawford measured samples of Peruvian thread against the modern scale of 840 yard hanks to the pound. Modern machine-spun Peruvian cotton ranges from number 50 to 70 while many of the ancient fibers were as high as 150 to 250. The same was true of the wools which measured two to three times the fineness of modern machine spun. Although single threads were used it was more common to twist two or more together before weaving.

The commonest loom was the back-strap type. It had two loom bars, one attached to a post, the other to a belt which went around the weaver's back and thus allowed control of the tension of the warp threads. The loom equipment was very simple. A cylindrical rod was used to separate one shed of alternate warps, and a simple form of heel rod or heddle for the other shed. The spindles served also as bobbins and the weft or fill was beaten up with a weave sword or short bone weave dagger. Smaller looms were used for belts and bands and there is indirect evidence for a frame loom since some of the fabrics are entirely too wide to be woven on the back-strap type.

Peruvian textiles can be grossly classified into two categories: plain weaves, in which both the warp and weft threads are visible on the finished surface; and repps or tapestries in which only the warp or the weft threads are visible. Further distinctions may be based on applied decorative techniques, such as embroidered or painted designs. In addition, there are the non-weaving techniques of netting, braiding, plaiting, crocheting, and knitting, which may be used by themselves or in combination with the weaving for finishing borders.

A detailed description of the numerous textile techniques used in ancient Peru would go far beyond the scope of this publication. (See J. Bird's section 3 in *Andean Culture History*, Bennett and Bird, American Museum of Natural History, 1949, and *Handbook of South American Indians*, Vol. I, Lila M. O'Neale.)

Fig. 131. Turban (knitted). Paracas Necropolis. 28′ long (unwound). Collection: Brooklyn Museum. (34.1594)

Left: Fig. 132. Mirror handle in shape of a deity holding two trophy heads. Chimu. Wood, 11⅝″ high. Collection: Ernest Erickson, courtesy Brooklyn Museum. (L. 42.87.16)

Below: Fig. 133. Small box, elaborately carved with bird designs. Coast Tiahuanaco. Wood, 9¼″ long. Collection: Norbert Mayrock, courtesy Museum für Völkerkunde, Munich

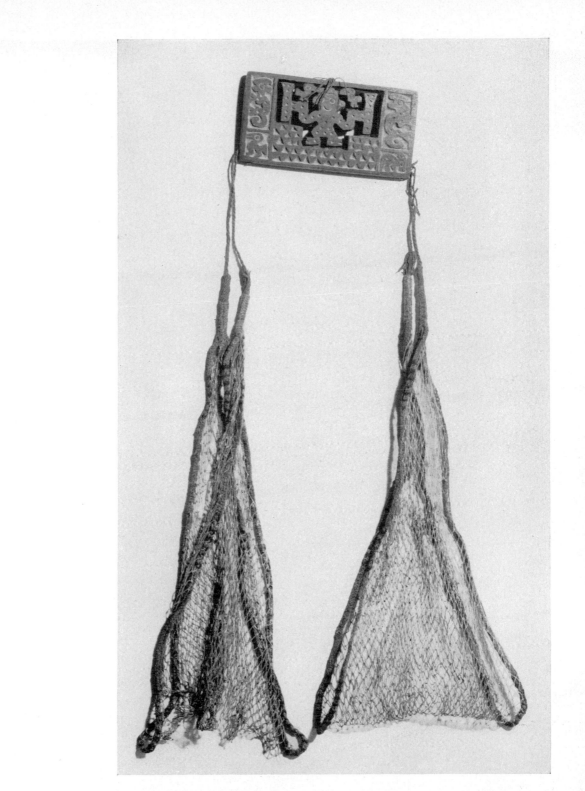

Fig. 134. Scales. Coast Tiahuanaco. Wood, 19⅝″ long. Collection: Brooklyn Museum (41.1275-126)

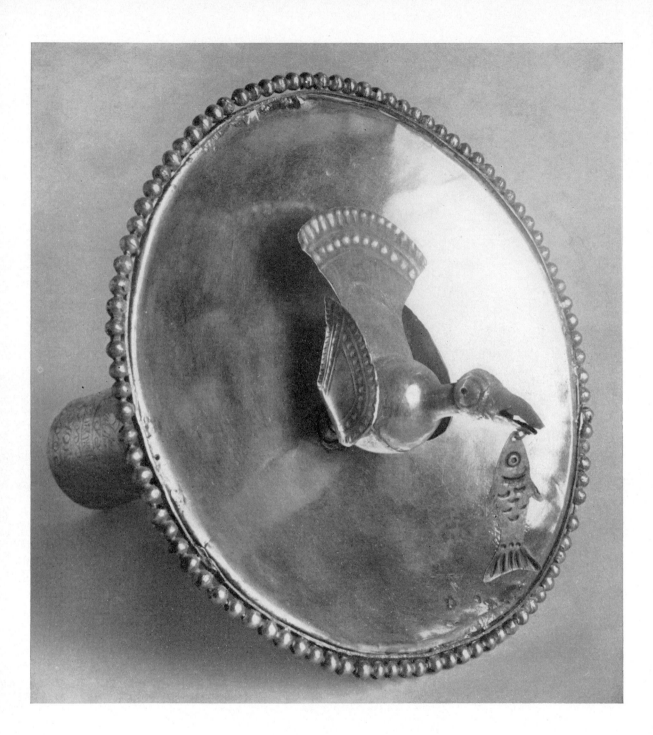

Fig. 135. Earplug. Chimu. Gold. Collection: Museo Nacional de Arqueología y Antropología, Peru

118

Fig. 136. Pendant. The design on the hand-shaped pendant represents a prisoner. Coast Tiahuanaco. Shell inlaid with turquoise and gold, 2½″ high. Collection: Norbert Mayrock, Santiago, Chile

Fig. 137. Front of a litter. Chimu. Wood, 37⅞″ wide. The Cleveland Museum of Art, John L. Severance Collection. (52.233)

Fig. 138. Earplug. Coast Tiahuanaco. Shell mosaic, 2⅝″ diameter. Collection: Dr. Eduard Gaffron, courtesy the Art Institute of Chicago

Fig. 139. Nose ornament. Nazca. Gold, 4″ high. Collection: Mr. and Mrs. René d'Harnoncourt

THE SOUTH

The Inca Empire in its southern extension incorporated the mountainous regions of northwest Argentina and an extensive part of modern Chile. There is ample archeological evidence in this southern region to confirm the Inca conquest. Well preserved sections of Inca roads are found in northwest Argentina, together with remains of rest houses, villages, and forts. The Inca polychrome ceramics, with characteristic aryballoid and dish shapes, are widely distributed and there are also typical lacquered goblets, stellate stone maces, and bronze knives and slit bells.

Prior to the Inca occupation, the southern cultures were essentially independent in their development although sharing many parallels with the Central Andes. The local cultures were distinctly Andean in that they depended on intensive agriculture, utilized irrigation systems, built extensively with rough stone, and manufactured ceramics, metal objects, and textiles. In spite of these parallels, the southern cultures were not merely an extension of the Central Andean, but have many characteristics of their own.

The South is sharply divided into an eastern and western section by the single range of Andes which separates modern Chile and Argentina. The population centers in

both sections are limited to a few intermont basins and river valleys. In north Chile, only the Rio Loa cuts through the Atacama desert and even it has but one large oasis, the Calama. Farther south, the small valleys in Coquimbo province supported some agricultural populations but the extensive central valley of Chile, today the garden spot of that country, was occupied by the warlike Araucanian hunters, who have resisted invasion with varying degrees of success, from the Inca time up to the present. In northwest Argentina there was only one major center for each of the present-day political provinces, namely, Jujuy, Salta, Tucumán, Catamarca, La Rioja, and Santiago del Estero. Each of these could support a fairly large agricultural population, and the surrounding puna highlands were suitable for herding llamas and alpacas.

Archeological work in the Southern Andes has been extensive but the coverage is spotty, so that the historical reconstructions are quite uneven.

Most of the pre-Inca archeological cultures in northwest Argentina and north Chile can be assigned to one of three major time periods, which correspond roughly to Periods Three, Four, and Five in the Central Andean sequence.

BARREALES

The early period is best represented by the Barreales culture centered principally in the province of Catamarca. The Barreales built simple houses of adobe and rough stone. Their ceramics are of two types. The first is a blackware with cups, pitchers, and bowls decorated with incised designs of pumas, birds, and human figures. The

Fig. 141. Urn. The form of the vessel is very handsome, but the crudeness of execution of the painted decoration contrasts with the intricacy of the design. Calchaquí. Clay, 22″ high. Collection: American Museum of Natural History. (41.0/642)

Opposite page: Fig. 140. Bowl, showing a wonderful use of fine line in both geometric and representional design. Calchaquí. Clay, 7″ diameter. Collection: American Museum of Natural History. (41.09451)

Fig. 142. Disk. Calchaquí. Bronze, 12″ diameter.
Collection: Chicago Museum of Natural History.
(100363)

second type is a polychrome ware, painted in black, maroon, and violet on a light-colored base. The design most often found is a curvilinear jaguar figure. The Barreales artisans also made quite a variety of stonework; clay effigy pipes; objects of gold and copper; and bone flutes and spatulas.

CALCHAQUÍ

The middle period, which corresponds roughly to the time of the Tiahuanaco expansion in the Central Andes, is dominated by the Calchaquí (or Diaguita) culture, found principally in Tucumán and Salta provinces but with ramifications everywhere. The Calchaquí lived in large villages with both round and rectangular rough stone houses, and built extensive irrigation systems and many stone-faced terraces. Geometrically carved stone columns were placed in some of the rooms perhaps as idols, but none of the constructions can be specifically identified as temples or religious centers.

Calchaquí had the unique practice of burying infants and children in polychrome painted urns in special cemeteries. The so-called Santa María urn is typical. It has a short, squat body with two side handles topped by tall flaring collar. The collar is decorated with a relief. Face, arms, and hands may be painted on the body of the vessel. The painted designs are in black, red, and white and consist of symmetrically arranged small panels with geometric steps and scrolls, or snakes, ostriches, toads, birds, and jaguars. Aside from the urns, there are many smaller vessels, such as ollas and open bowls, decorated with similar colors and designs. Variants on this style are found in most parts of northwest Argentina. Across the mountains, the local Chilean Diaguita culture presents many of the same ceramic features, although the vessels are more

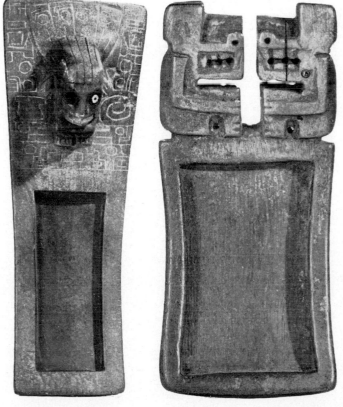

Left: Fig. 144. Snuff tablet. Atacameño. Related in style to Tiahuanaco carvings. Wood, 6″. Collection: American Museum of Natural History. (41.0/8911)

Right: Fig. 145. Snuff tablet. Atacameño. Related in style to Tiahuanaco carvings. Wood, 6¼″ high. Collection: American Museum of Natural History. (41.0/8754)

Opposite: Fig. 143. Plaque. Calchaquí. Bronze, c. 6½″ wide. Collection: Museum of the American Indian, Heye Foundation

125

precisely painted and the urns too small to have been used for purposes of burial.

Although quite a variety of artifacts were made by the Calchaquí only the cast copper and bronze objects are particularly distinctive. These include curved knives, daggers, and knuckle dusters but the most outstanding are cast plaques, with reliefs of standing human figures flanked with jaguars, or highly stylized human faces.

ATACAMEÑO

The cultures of the late period, prior to the Inca invasion, show, like the Peruvian counterparts, increased emphasis on political and military organization and a general reduction of craftsmanship to the utilitarian level. The Atacameño culture is an exception, and quite unique. In their homeland on the Calama oasis of North Chile, the Atacameño may have existed for many years prior to this late period, and in any case they persisted into the Spanish times. The Atacameño were principally travelers and traders using herds of llamas as pack animals. There is evidence for their extension into northwest Argentina and other parts of Chile. Their graves contain many wooden objects, such as toggles for the cinch belts of the llama harness, wooden bells with wooden clappers, decorated boxes, carved tablets and tubes for snuff, goblets, knives, and shovels. In the Calama oasis there have been found artifacts of almost pure Tiahuanaco manufacture, ceramics similar to those of southern Peru, and obvious trade pieces from the Coquimbo region of Chile. If the Atacameño were, as the evidence suggests, great traders and travelers this would account for the mixture.

Fig. 146. Bat god. Esmeraldas, Ecuador. Gold, 9½″ wide. Collection: University Museum, Philadelphia. (SA 2833)

THE NORTH

The prehistoric cultures of the Central Andes formed a fairly compact unit over a considerable period of time. In the northern Andes there was no such unity, either geographically or culturally. The North covers the mountainous sections and coastal plains of the modern countries of Ecuador, Colombia, Venezuela, Panama, and Costa Rica, which were as diverse in the past as they are today. There is no evidence that this extensive area was ever united politically nor are there widespread styles which would imply some form of cultural unity. In part this picture of disunity may be due to the lack of sufficient archeological knowledge, but it also appears to reflect the nature of the development of the northern Andean cultures.

In the pre-Spanish periods, the inhabitable areas of the North are more limited than in the Central Andes. Ecuador, to be sure, has a series of highland basins between its two parallel mountain ranges but these are for the most part badly eroded and with thin soils. There is only one sizeable highland basin in Colombia, around the capital city of Bogotá, and this was occupied by the Chibcha who, according to the early Spanish accounts, had a fairly complex civilization. Elsewhere in Colombia there are only small, isolated basins and limited sections of river flats which could be occupied by the prehistoric, agricultural people. In Peru, the major contemporary centers of population correspond closely to those of the past but this is not true in Colombia where many new centers have been made possible by such post-Spanish introductions as bananas, coffee, sheep, cattle, sugar cane, and oil.

The northern coastal plains along the Pacific and the Caribbean are mainly tropical. Actually, the tropics and the highlands are in fairly close juxtaposition since the tropical forest follows up some of the larger river valleys like the Atrato and the Magdalena. Hence, the highland cultures show considerable tropical influence.

By and large, the northern cultures did not build with permanent materials and did not construct large temples or public buildings. There are, to be sure, some exceptions, like the large earthen mounds in northern Ecuador, the subterranean stone-lined temple chambers of San Agustín in Colombia, and extensive stone buildings of the Tairona culture in Santa Marta. On the other hand, cultures like the Chibcha have not left any spectacular surface ruins.

The wet forest coverage on the highland slopes is not suitable for grazing the llamas and alpacas. As a consequence, the weavers had only cotton for fibers, and the textile art was not too advanced. Instead, the best developed crafts were ceramics, stone-work, and metallurgy, and of these the skilled work in gold is the most outstanding.

The North developed several political and social patterns but none leading to super-states and empire building. The religious patterns are difficult to judge since ceremonial centers and temples are not common, but some of the cultures made idols of

Fig. 147. Small mask representing the bat god with feline teeth. Ecuador. Gold, 2¾″ high. Collection: The Cleveland Museum of Art, Gift of Mrs. Henry Norweb. (50.414)

wood or gold, and all had elaborate graves which contain quantities of fine offerings.

In spite of the lack of over-all unity and certain limitations of craftsmanship, the cultures of the North should not be considered as poor cousins of those of the Central Andes. In many ways, they show distinctive developments and cultural independence. Influences from the Central Andes are present, but hard to interpret. A chronology is exceptionally difficult to establish in the North, due largely to the limited amount of archeological work.

Because the northern cultures are so regionally isolated and because there is still no satisfactory over-all chronology, each major culture must be described separately, although it is possible to suggest external affiliations. For convenience of presentation the cultures are arranged in terms of modern political divisions.

Opposite: Fig. 148. Crown. Sigsig, Ecuador. Gold, c. 22″ high. Collection: Museum of the American Indian, Heye Foundation. (1/2062)

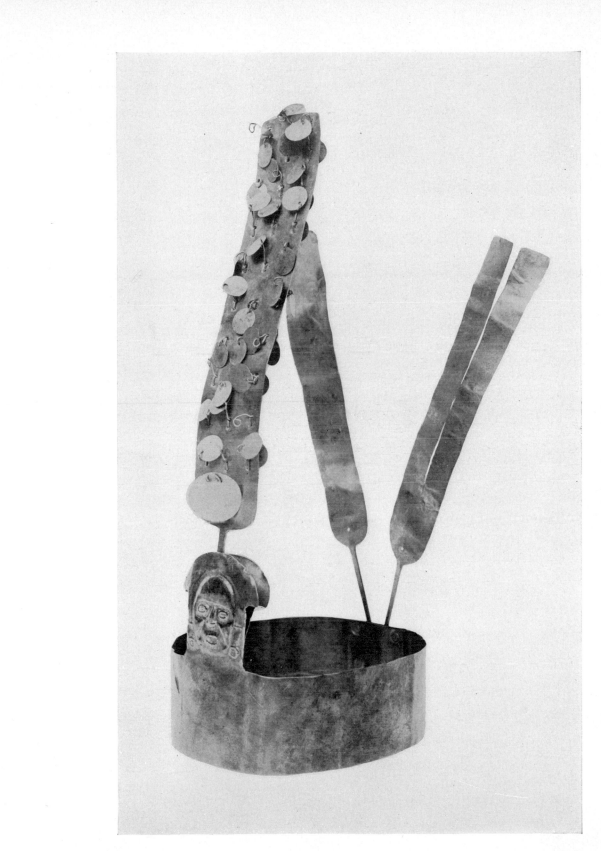

Fig. 149. Vessel in shape of a feline. These monumental animal figures are unique in style in South America. Carchi. Clay, 17⅞″ high. Collection: Brooklyn Museum. (39.279)

ECUADOR

CAÑAR AND AZUAY

In the south highlands, in the provinces of Cañar and Azuay, gold and gilded copper objects have been found in abundance. These include decorated plates, discs, bells, and many types of ornaments. The ceramics show a mixture of styles, of which the best known is a highly polished red-on-buff, both modeled and engraved. There are also clay cylinders which have been called drums or seats. Some have seen Mayan influence in these ceramics, but actually the culture seems highly local.

Fig. 150. Urn decorated with negative painting. It is possible that these slender urns are related to the Inca aryballos. Carchi. Clay, 28½″ high. Collection: University Museum, Philadelphia. (29-51-121)

Fig. 151. Pectoral or head ornament. The animal designs surrounding the head are closely allied with designs from Central America. Esmeraldas. Hammered gold, 14″ wide. Collection: University Museum, Philadelphia. (SA 2831)

CARCHI

In the northernmost basin, next to the Colombian border, the Carchi culture used large, circular earthen walls for the foundations of their conical frame houses, and buried their dead in deep shaft graves with side chambers. The graves contain many small stone artifacts, such as well polished axes, and great quantities of ceramic vessels. Two styles characterize the ceramics. One is a polished redware, particularly noted for its modeled animals. The other is three-color negative ware. The most typical shape is an elongated, narrow jar with conical base and tall flaring collar. The style of negative painting is like that of the Tuncahuán horizon which corresponds roughly to Period Four in the Central Andes. (See Fig. 150.)

ESMERALDAS

Although the northern coast of Ecuador lies in the tropics, the archeological remains are numerous. Large earthen mounds, as many as forty in a group, serve both for burial and habitation, but there is no stone building or stone carving. There are, however, numerous small stone artifacts such as axes, ring stones, polishers, and grinders. Esmeraldas is noted for its gold ornaments and its large copper discs and gongs, decorated with high-relief animal and human figures.

The ceramics are highly varied from large vessels to some small enough to be called miniatures. Most vessels are plain ware but others are decorated with red paint, incisions, and modeled lugs. Both large and small clay figurines are the outstanding characteristic of Esmeraldas culture. The large ones represent seated figures with the legs straight out or with the knees drawn up. The small ones show excellent modeling and their style of headdress and other details is reminiscent of the Maya of Central America. On the other hand, the relief designs on the cylindrical and flat clay stamps suggest the Chavín style of Peru.

Fig. 152. Pectoral or head ornament representing the bat god flanked by four human figures. Esmeraldas. Hammered gold, 13½″ wide. Collection: University Museum, Philadelphia (SA 2832)

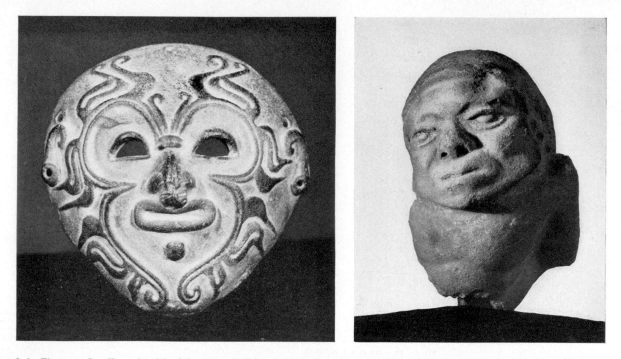

Left: Fig. 153. Small mask with elaborate relief decorations. Esmeraldas. Clay, 5½" high. Collection: Brooklyn Museum (35.1860) *Right:* Fig. 154. Fragment of a figurine representing a hunchback. Esmeraldas. Clay, 3⅜" high. Collection: Brooklyn Museum. (35.1859)

MANABÍ

The Esmeraldas culture is surprisingly advanced for tropical forest dwellers and the Manabí culture, in the next province to the south, is equally so. This region is transitional between the tropical and desert zones but is nonetheless heavily forested. Manabí is the only Ecuadorean culture which built extensively with stone. There are stone-faced platform mounds, clusters of walled house units, enclosures and bottle-shaped tombs cut into the natural rock. In addition, the Manabí were stone carvers. They carved simple statues, like modified columns, plaques with low-relief figures enclosed within geometrically designed panels, and large U-shaped stone seats which rest on crouching animals or human figures. The carving style has been compared with that of Tiahuanaco in Bolivia although there is no good evidence for historical connections. The ceramics, like those of Esmeraldas, are varied in shapes and decorations. Manabí likewise has large and small clay figurines although not so well modeled as those of Esmeraldas.

The affiliations of Esmeraldas and Manabí with both Central America and Peru would imply wide scale trade, and the first Spaniards were impressed by the abilities of these coastal Ecuadorean peoples as navigators. They made large rafts of balsa logs, capable of distant journeys.

134

Fig. 155. Seat, monumental in form and reminiscent of the stone work of Central America. Manabí. Stone, 28½″ high. Collection: American Museum of Natural History. (41.0/395)

Fig. 156. Amulet. Quimbaya. Gold, 2⅞″ high. Collection: The Cleveland Museum of Art, Gift of Mrs. Henry Norweb. (39.509)

COLOMBIA

SAN AGUSTÍN

The headwaters of the Magdalena River lie in the rolling mountains of southern Colombia. The hills are forest covered, and there are high peaks, and deep cut-out gorges. It is not an area of large population today and probably was about the same in the past. Nonetheless, it was the center of the unique San Agustín culture noted for its quantity and variety of stone carving, subterranean stone-lined temples and stone box tombs. The numerous statues and constructions are not concentrated in one small area but rather spread throughout a large section of this forested region. Over three hundred stone carvings have been described, ranging from carved boulders to immense statues with human features and crossed fangs. San Agustín may well correspond in time to Period Two in the Central Andes, but it may also have been in existence over a long time span.

Fig. 157. Stela. San Agustín. Stone

The most elaborate constructions are artificial, earthen mounds, some as much as 80 feet in diameter and 14 feet high, which contain subterranean temples, walled and roofed with enormous stone slabs. Each temple has at least one principal and several subsidiary idols. There are also smaller constructions of the same type, called shrines, stone-lined subterranean galleries, and box-like burial vaults.

The stone carvings and temples are so outstanding that other aspects of San Agustín culture have been largely ignored. The ceramics are drab, monochrome ollas and open bowls, decorated by simple incisions.

San Agustín remains a mystery. The numerous shrines and idols imply strong religious motivation but their scattered distribution throughout the forest would suggest local cult practices rather than formal organization.

TIERRADENTRO

The territory between the headwaters of the Magdalena and the Cauca Rivers is called Tierradentro and is about the same kind of forested hill country as the San

Fig. 158. Interior of tomb cut in the rock, painted with geometric designs and conventionalized heads. The similarity of these designs to the decoration on Chibcha pottery (for example see Fig. 176) is striking. Tierradentro

Fig. 159. Vessel surmounted by three figures, decorated with negative painting. Quimbaya. Clay, 14″ high. Collection: University Museum, Philadelphia. (SA 4614)

Agustín region. Actually, a few stone statues and stone-lined tombs of San Agustín type are found in the area.

Tierradentro culture itself is best known for its painted, subterranean burial chambers. These were cut out of the soft rock and not reinforced by walls or other construction work. The chamber is entered by means of a spiral staircase with irregular steps, which descends to the floor level, as much as 18 feet below the ground surface. The oval-shaped chamber, from 12 to 30 feet long, has an arched roof, one or more central pillars, and inset niches in the walls. Niches, walls, roof, and central columns are completely decorated with high-relief figures and with painted black, red, and white geometric designs. The chambers contain no complete ceramic vessels, but the floors are covered with broken pieces of thick vessels, decorated by appliqué, punching, incised lines with a white paste, and, rarely, two-color negative painting.

The Tierradentro culture is found only in this area, and like San Agustín there is no particular concentration at any one site. Evidence for final time placement is lacking but Tierradentro is probably later than San Agustín.

QUIMBAYA

The Quimbaya lived on the middle Cauca River in what is now the state of Antioquia. They left us no ruins of village sites, ceremonial centers, or agricultural terraces. If it were not for their graves, the Quimbaya would be a forgotten people.

The graves, fortunately, are numerous and richly stocked with offerings. They are usually of the shaft and side-chamber type. The shafts are circular or square and range in depth up to thirty or more feet. The burials are extended on the chamber floor surrounded by pottery, stone tools, and the fabulous gold ornaments which have so famed the Quimbaya and so inspired the clandestine excavators.

The ceramic vessels are numerous, quite varied in shapes and designs but not particularly outstanding in quality. There are open bowls, double bowls with modeled bird or animal containers, tall jars with angular shoulders, pedestal bowls, tripod and tetrapod jars, and large and small figurine jars. Some vessels are painted in black,

Left: Fig. 160. Miniature stirrup-spout jar with snake head, decorated with an exquisite carving, comparable in workmanship with Quimbaya goldsmith work. Quimbaya. Clay, 3½″ high. Collection: American Museum of Natural History. (40/913) *Center:* Fig. 161. Seated figure with raised arm, decorated with negative painting. Quimbaya. Clay, 12⅝″ high. Collection: Brooklyn Museum. (38.613) *Right:* Fig. 162. Vessel in shape of a bird. Quimbaya. Clay, 8″ high. Collection: Chicago Natural History Museum. (65097). The fabulous variety in style and quality of execution of the five ceramics shown on pages 139, 140, and 141 suggest the existence of several well-defined culture periods in the region.

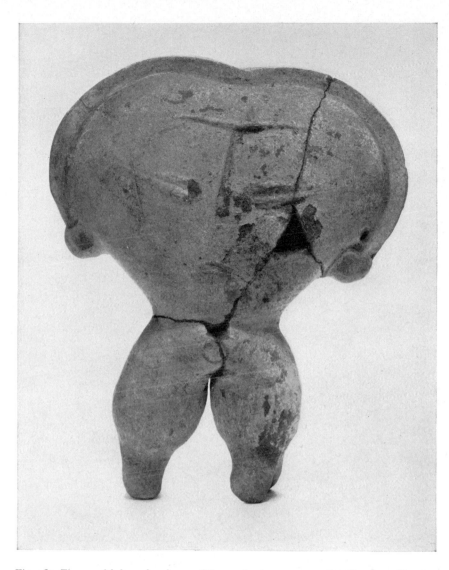

Fig. 163. Figure with huge head, one of the most extreme conventionalizations of human beings in South American archeology. Quimbaya, Clay, 9¼″ high. Collection: American Museum of Natural History. (40/611)

white, and red, but the characteristic decoration is two- and three-color negative painting, which links the Quimbaya to the Tuncahuán of Ecuador and in general to Period Four in the Central Andes. Other decorative techniques are modeling, incision, appliqué and the champlevé type of cut-out background.

Cloth itself is not preserved, but the numerous clay spindle whorls indicate a knowledge of spinning and weaving. There are also several types of carved clay stamps for decorating cloth or the body. The stone artifacts include T-shaped axes, polished adzes, grindstones, and tubular beads. However, the greatest technical and artistic

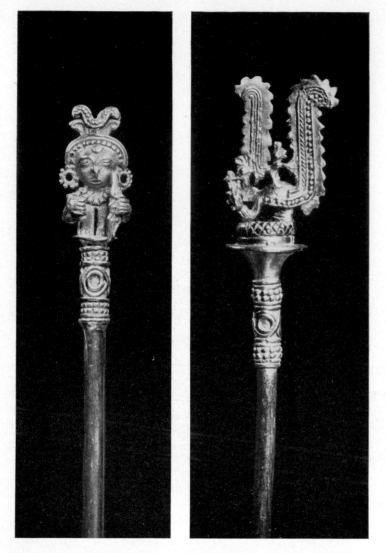

Left: Fig. 164. Pin. Quimbaya. Gold, 8 15/16″ long. Collection: The Cleveland Museum of Art, J. H. Wade Collection. (47.30) *Right:* Fig. 165. Pin. Quimbaya. Gold, 15¾″ long. Collection: The Cleveland Museum of Art, gift of Mrs. B. P. Bole. (46.461)

Opposite above: Fig. 166. Large breastplate, hammered gold with repoussé decoration. Antioquia. 22″ wide. Collection: University Museum, Philadelphia. (SA 2701) *Below:* Fig. 167. Breastplate. Antioquia. Gold, 12″ diameter. Collection: University Museum, Philadelphia. (SA 2704)

142

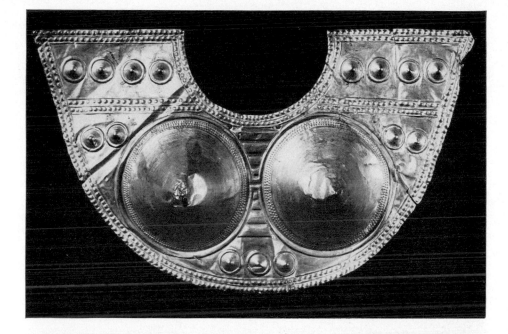

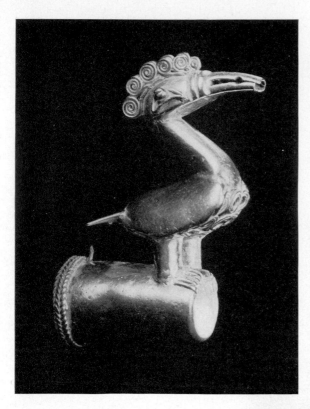

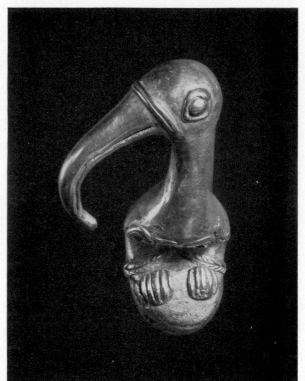

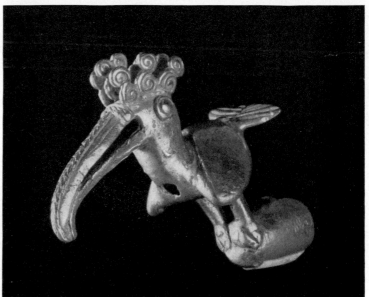

Above left: Fig. 168. Staff finial. Quimbaya. Gold, 4⅝″ high. Collection: Nelson A. Rockefeller

Above right: Fig. 169. Mace head. Quimbaya. Gold, 3½″ high. Collection: John Wise, New York

Right: Fig. 170. Mace Head. Quimbaya. Gold, 3¼″ high. Collection: The Cleveland Museum of Art, Mr. and Mrs. Henry Humphreys Memorial. (47.25)

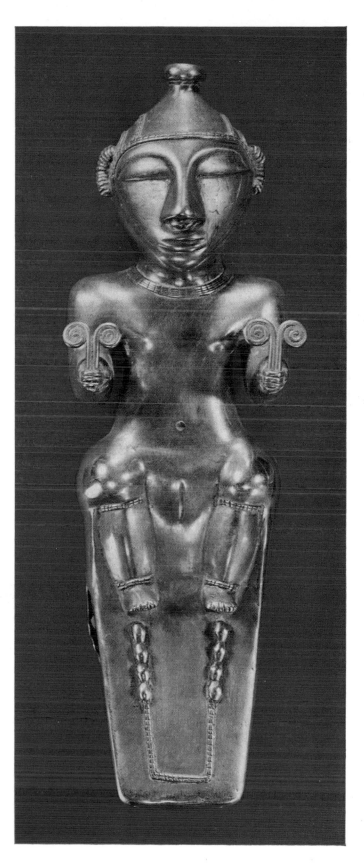

Fig. 171. Seated figure holding spiral ornaments,
molded by the *cire perdue* process. Quimbaya.
Gold, 9″ high. Collection University Museum,
Philadelphia (SA 2751). Photo Nickolas Muray

Fig. 172. Group of objects which are the finest examples of South American goldsmith art. Quimbaya. Gold. Collection: Museo Arqueológico de Madrid

achievement of the Quimbaya was in metallurgy, and their skill in casting gold ornaments is truly surprising in view of the general simplicity of other aspects of the culture.

The available metals were limited to gold, or the gold-copper alloy called *tumbaga*, but these were fabricated into ornaments and objects by hammering, repoussé, cutout, cast filigree, solid and hollow casting, and soldering. Variations were achieved by joining bands of metal of slightly different composition. Many of the objects were ornaments: earrings, nose rings, bracelets, beads, diadems, breast plates, and necklaces. They also made masks, and ornamented scepters, vases, idols, figurines, and beautifully shaped bottles, decorated with relief figures. The bottles are particularly noted for their exquisite form and simplicity of outline. In both technique and quality the Quimbaya gold work is unequalled in the Andean region.

Fig. 174. Seated warrior. The violent distortions of the figure suggest the possibility of a consciously grotesque treatment of the subject. Upper Cauca region. Clay, 15" high. Collection: A. F. Tower, on loan to the American Museum of Natural History. (T34-1A&B)

SINÚ

The Sinú River cuts its way northward to the Caribbean through heavy tropical forest. Although the early Spaniards reported large earthen mounds, no scientific work has ever been done in this region. The few Sinú pieces which have been acquired by museums include some heavy gold objects of simple design, and some ceramic vessels and bowls often decorated with figurines in high relief. One pedestal base is ornamented with high-relief, male and female figures which have tattooed bodies and wear short skirts and breech clouts of tropical type. There is no evidence for the time placement of these few finds.

UPPER CAUCA

On the upper Cauca River, between the towns of Cali and Popayán, shaft-and-chamber graves have been found which contain great quantities of monochrome redware ollas and pedestal jars, ornamented with appliqué relief. These show little relationship with the Quimbaya ceramics to the north and presumably represent a culture later in time. No construction work is found, although simple terraces cut out on the hill slopes served as bases for house sites. The most elaborate clay objects represent seated modeled warriors, with shields and comb-like headdresses of a peculiar imaginative savagery.

NARIÑO

In the southwest corner of Colombia, next to the Ecuadorian border, the Nariño culture is known largely through local collections of grave objects. Although these include some small stone tools and ornaments and some simple gold pieces, they are largely ceramic. The style is quite consistent, and closely related to the neighboring Ecuadorian Carchi. The commonest vessel shapes are open bowls and plates, many with pedestal bases. The geometric and simple monkey designs are executed in three-color negative technique in black, white, and red. There are also clay ocarinas painted in red on cream.

MOSQUITO

Large burial urns have been found at the hacienda Mosquito, located in the tropical forests which cover the banks of the middle Magdalena River. The urns are tall cylindrical jars with appliqué relief animal figures on the side. Each urn has a cover on which sits an enormous modeled figure, either male or female, with slit eyes, relief nose, and hands resting on the knees. Arms and legs show ligatures of Amazonian type. The Mosquito culture, if it can be so designated, is known only by these urns.

TAIRONA

The isolated mountain range of Santa Marta in the northeast corner of Colombia was the home of the Tairona culture, truly exceptional because of its numerous surface remains. The elaborate village sites have circular house foundations, lined with

dressed-stone blocks; stone platform house sites; stone-faced mounds; large ceremonial courts; and a profusion of stone steps, roads, paths, slab bridges, and reservoirs. The burials are found in urns, in unlined pits, and in dressed-stone vaults.

The ceramics fall into two categories, a blackware and a redware. The blackware is represented by pedestal bowls, collar jars, modeled vessels with stirrup spouts, and double-spout jars. The redware is largely limited to bowls, plates, and jars.

Tairona culture is also noted for its stone artifacts, which include utilitarian grind-stones, mortars, pestles, and ring stones and also finely finished and polished stone and jade batons, broad-winged pendants, miniature seats or tables, and a great variety of beads and figurines. The metalwork consists of gold, or the gold-copper alloy, beads, rings, pendants, bells, and batons, made by hammering, repoussé, hollow casting, and soldering.

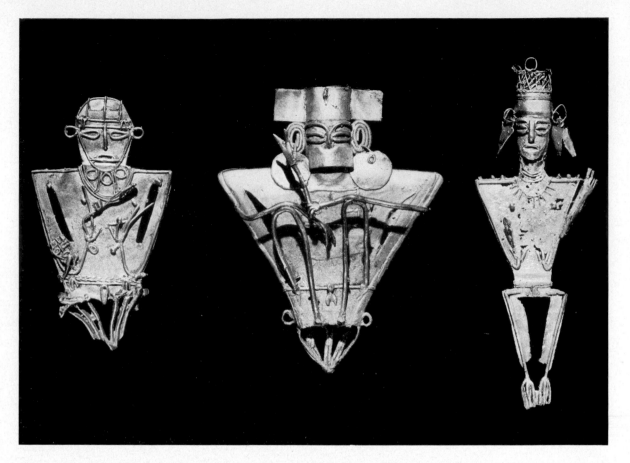

Fig. 177. Three figures. In contrast with the three-dimensional figures of the Quimbaya region, Chibcha figurines are based on a flat contour overlayed with gold wire often resembling a line drawing. They are highly stylized and show great variety and imagination. Chibcha. Cast gold. *Left:* 3¾″ high (6600) *Center:* 4¼″ high (6620) *Right:* 4⅞″ high (6706). Collection: Chicago Natural History Museum

CHIBCHA

The Chibcha who inhabited the large highland basin around Bogotá was the only culture described in any detail by the conquering Spaniards. Throughout the years the early accounts may have become somewhat exaggerated but nonetheless the basic pattern seems essentially correct. The high basin of Bogotá was the best in Colombia for pre-Columbian agriculture. Many estimates have been made of the size of the Chibcha population, some running up to a million, but careful analysis indicates that 300,000 would be about the maximum population.

The Chibcha agricultural techniques and domesticated plants were similar to those elsewhere in the Andes, but it is still debated whether or not irrigation was practiced. Although in some parts of Colombia the clothing pattern was like that of the Amazon,

Fig. 178. Three figures. Chibcha. Cast gold. *Left:* 4″ high (47.22) *Center:* 5¼″ high (47.18) *Right:* 3¹¹⁄₁₆″ high (47.23). Collection: The Cleveland Museum of Art, Mr. and Mrs. Henry Humphreys Memorial

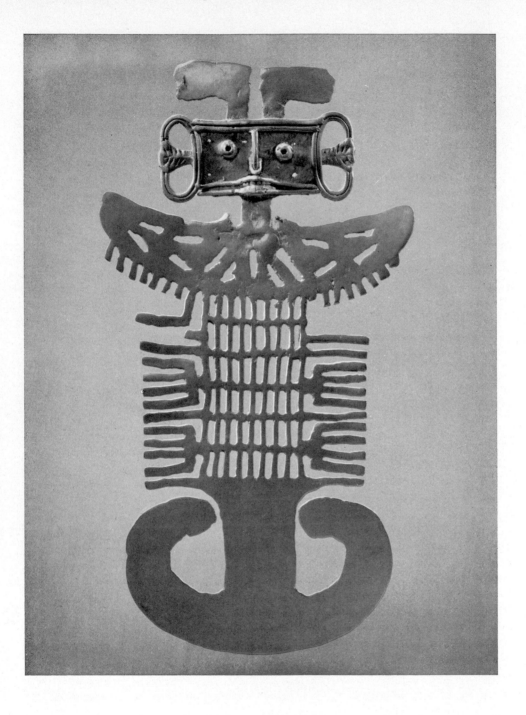

Fig. 179. Ceremonial knife. Chibcha. Cast gold, 7″ high. Collection: University Museum, Philadelphia. (SA 2753)

Fig. 180. Ceremonial knife. Cast gold, 7″ high. Collection: University Museum, Philadelphia. (SA 2754)

the Chibcha wore the standard slit-neck shirts, breech clouts, skirts, and shawls of the Andean type.

The houses are described as circular with conical roofs, made of wood frame and thatch. The Chibcha made tools of stone and wood, competent ceramics, wove cotton cloth, and cast gold and copper into ornaments and figurines.

Chibcha society was divided into two classes, nobles and commoners, with the warriors as a special group. The political organization had reached the stage of local states, which were sometimes loosely united into confederacies. The state was headed by an absolute monarch, called the Zipa, who was treated with great respect and special ceremony. He was carried about in a litter and seated on a throne of gold. The office was inherited through the female line. The noble class was supported by the warrior group which was composed of selected youths from the commoners. The warriors used special dress and had many special privileges.

The priesthood was loosely organized but not as a hierarchy. Again the office was inherited in the female line. The priests resided at temples, similar to ordinary huts but containing sacred idols, where they served as diviners and intermediaries between the people and the gods. The idols were made of wood, clay, and gold, and usually used in pairs, one male and one female, sometimes combined in the same figure. Parrots, slaves, and selected children were sacrificed to these idols, particularly at the special ceremonies held at harvest time and on the occasion of the inauguration of a new ruler.

The Chibcha gods show many parallels with those of the Maya and Aztec of Central America. Foremost among them was Bochica, the white-bearded culture hero whose attributes are like those of the Mayan Quetzalcoatl. The gods were departmentalized, that is, each had charge of certain types of activity. For example, the god Nencatocoa was in charge of drinking, weaving, and designers. This is like the Aztec god Macuil-Xochipilli who was in charge of amusement, weaving, and artists.

The political and religious systems, particularly the concept of gods, show many parallels to the Aztecs and Maya but otherwise the Chibcha compare closely with the Central Andean pattern prior to the superimposition of the Inca political structure.

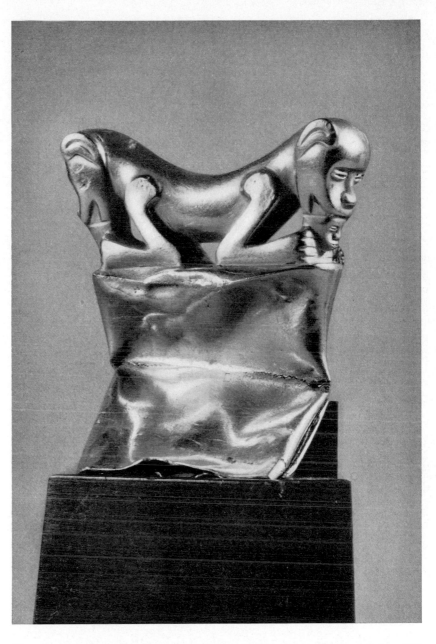

Fig. 181. Staff head with double-headed puma. Colombia or Panama. Gold, 3¼″ high. Collection: The Cleveland Museum of Art, The J. H. Wade Fund. (44.319)

VENEZUELA

The Andes of Venezuela, like Colombia, contain a number of regional cultures with little evidence of widespread unity and still no satisfactory time sequences. The emphasis on stone artifacts, particularly beads and bat-wing pendants, as well as the common employment of low relief and appliqué in ceramic decoration links Venezuela with Colombia, but the differences are still great.

At a site called La Mata, on the shores of Lake Valencia, there is evidence of a lacustrine population who once built their houses on piles over the shallows of the lake. They also constructed mounds of earth in which they interred their dead either directly or in large clay urns. The accompanying ceramics are red or grey bowls, decorated with modeled adornos. Modeled clay figurines are especially characteristic. The squat bodies have enormous heads, either oval or canoe-shaped, and the figures are decidedly steatopygous. Occasionally more realistic figurines with sensitive modeling are found.

Fig. 182. Seated woman. Venezuela. Clay, 6½″ high. Collection: American Museum of Natural History. (41.0/2735)

Fig. 183. Figure of a deity. The relationship of this piece to realistic Quimbaya figures is evident in the treatment of the body. However, the elaborate and stylized rendering of head and headdress are of unique complexity. La Guaira, Venezuela. Gold, c. 5″ high. Collection: Robert Woods Bliss, courtesy The National Gallery of Art, Washington, D.C.

PANAMA AND COSTA RICA

The highlands and tropical forests of Panama and Costa Rica present many independent regional cultures. The abundance of small stone artifacts and gold work is similar to Colombia, but Central American cultures show greater elaboration of surface construction and stone carving which may reflect northern influences.

Fig. 184. Plaque in shape of a human face with feline teeth. This piece, in its simplicity, recalls the style of Central American stone carving rather than the fluid styles of most other gold work. Coclé. Gold, 3¾" high. Collection: The Cleveland Museum of Art, gift of Mrs. Henry Norweb. (51.155)

Fig. 185. Helmet representing the crocodile god. Coclé. Gold, c. 6″ wide. Collection: Peabody Museum, Harvard University. (227½13045-25)

COCLÉ

The uplands of Panama supported fairly advanced local cultures in the years just preceding the conquest. The elaborate burials of the Coclé culture, southwest of the Canal, are the best known. These are of large size with a central stone slab on which the principal deceased was placed. A single grave may contain over two hundred pottery vessels and many other artifacts of stone and gold. The most typical vessels are

159

curved-bottom plates and bowls, decorated in five to six colors. Modeled vessels are also common. There are many stone objects, such as grindstones, jade pendants, and polished stone beads. Gold objects are of excellent quality and include headbands, discs, nose rings, and other ornaments.

Fig. 186. Plaque representing the crocodile god. Coclé. Gold, c. 12″ wide. Collection: Peabody Museum, Harvard University. (225½13045-263)

Fig. 187. Pendant representing the bat god. Ivory and gold, 5½″ high. Collection: Peabody Museum, Harvard University. (13045-143)

Fig. 188. Pendant in form of an insect. Coclé. Gold and quartz, 2″ long. Collection: Peabody Museum, Harvard University. (33-42-20/1777)

Fig. 189. Pendant in form of a fantastic animal. Coclé. Gold and emerald, 4½″ long. Collection: University Museum, Philadelphia (40-13-27)

Above: Fig. 190. Bottle with painted design on neck. Coclé. Clay, c. 7″ high. Collection: Peabody Museum, Harvard University. (10867) *Below:* Fig. 191. Plate on stand, decorated with a relatively simple figure of the crocodile god. Coclé. Clay, 7¾″ diameter. Collection: Peabody Museum, Harvard University. (33-42-20/1589)

CHIRIQUÍ

In northern Panama, the local collectors have assembled many objects from graves in the Chiriquí province. These include cast gold ornaments, similar in quality and technique to the Quimbaya; ornamental jaguar metates or grindstones with animal legs; rare stone statues; and negative-painted pottery which presents a variety of tripod types.

164

Opposite page: Fig. 192. Plate, decorated with a very complex representation of the crocodile god. A fine example of composite design. Coclé. Clay, 14⅜″ diameter. Collection: Heeramaneck Galleries

Fig. 193. Anthropomorphic figure with animal features. Chiriquí. Stone, 34½″ high. Collection: Brooklyn Museum. (37.2894L)

Fig. 194. Pendant. This represents the most abstract form of goldwork in the Americas. Only by comparison with other pieces is it possible to ascertain that the two small knobs resembling screw heads represent the eyes of a figure and the spirals between them its nose. Chiriquí. Gold, 7½″ high. Collection: The Museum of the Cranbrook Academy of Art. (1947.9)

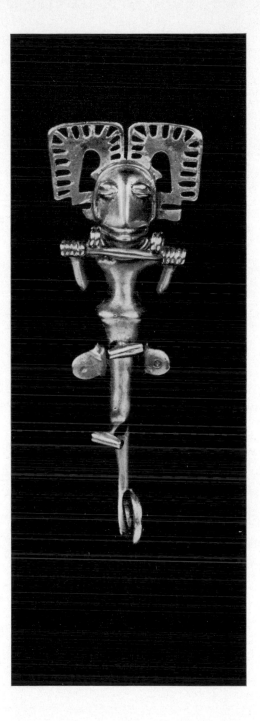

Fig. 195. Pendant representing a fantastic animal. Veraguas, Panama. Gold, 3½" high. Collection: The Cleveland Museum of Art, Mr. and Mrs. Henry Humphreys Memorial. (43.287)

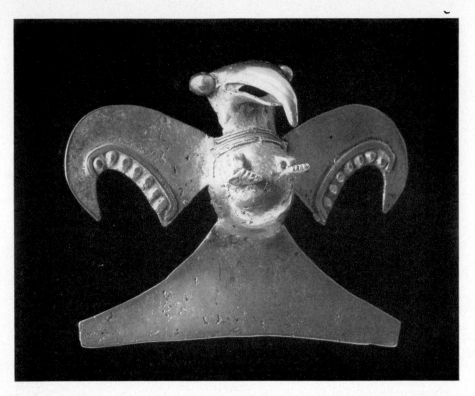

Fig. 196. Pendant representing an eagle. Veraguas. Gold, 3½″ high. Collection: Nelson A. Rockefeller.

Fig. 197. Pendant representing a frog. Nicoya, Costa Rica. Gold, 1⅜″ high. Collection: Brooklyn Museum. (35.214)

NICOYA

On the Pacific side of Costa Rica, the Nicoya occupied the peninsula of the same name. The Nicoya erected earthen and stone-faced mounds, and carved column-like stone statues representing both human and animal figures with angular relief limbs and features.

The Nicoya buried in pit graves and urns. Their ceramics are of exceptionally fine quality. The Nicoya polychrome is characterized by pear-shaped containers, with annular or tripod bases, painted in bright colors with designs which appear to be geometric but which in reality are highly conventionalized animals. The Nicoya alligator ware is so named because the bowl covers are modeled into alligator figures.

Fig. 198. Pendant representing a fantastic animal. Nicoya, Costa Rica. Gold, 3⅞″ high. Collection: Brooklyn Museum. (35.148)

Fig. 199. Grinding stone. Costa Rica. 17¼″ long. Collection: Heeramaneck Galleries

The Nicoya also made good quality gold ornaments, and many stone artifacts, such as maces, club heads, bark beaters, and jade ornaments. Their large ceremonial grinding stones are the most characteristic. These have three or four legs, a projecting animal head, and a curled tail, and are decorated on the sides with an incised geometric pattern. They may well have been used as seats or benches.

THE EAST

The great expanse of tropical jungle which extends from the eastern slopes of the Andes to the Atlantic was as an effective block to the expansion of the Inca Empire. In earlier periods, however, the contrasts between the Andean and the tropical forest cultures may not have been so great. At least, a number of Amazonian traits occur in the early periods of the Central Andean sequence, for example, bark cloth, blowguns, and feather fans; parrots and armadillos; peanuts and manioc, both tropical forest plants. Some scholars have even suggested that the Chavín culture was essentially Amazonian, and that its curvilinear style of stone sculpture was derived from wood carving.

Fig. 200. Bowl with painted and incised decoration. Marajão, Brazil. Clay, 17½″ wide. Collection: American Museum of Natural History. (41.0/1425)

Fig. 201. *Tanga*, painted ceramic triangle which was worn like a fig-leaf by Marajão women. Marajão, Brazil. Clay, 5¼″ high. Collection: American Museum of Natural History. (4.0/1391)

Archeological work in Amazonia has not been very extensive. The few known sites are widely scattered throughout the vast region and cannot be properly placed in a time sequence. Some of the forest sites in eastern Bolivia show Tiahuanaco influences corresponding to Period Four in the Central Andes, and although the Amazon region must have been occupied long before this, proof is lacking.

Three widely separated sites along the Amazon River banks share certain stylistic features and may represent a common cultural horizon. The first, Marajão, is located on the periodically flooded islands in the mouth of the Amazon. Over a hundred large earthen mounds have been discovered which contain urn burials. The urns are of the effigy type with crude representations of human figures. They are decorated by incision, relief, and positive painting in red, brown, and white. The designs are geometric or highly stylized animals. The characteristic pattern is that of alternating broad and fine lines. The mounds also contain many jars and bowls, decorated like the urns, several types of clay figurines, and curved triangular clay pieces, called *tangas*, which were worn by the women for protection in the water.

The second site, Mirakanguéra, is located on the middle Amazon at the juncture of the Madeira River, and again is represented by effigy urns. The arms and legs of the

Fig. 202. Large burial urn, with painted and modeled decorations. Marajão, Brazil. Clay, c. 4′ high. Collection: Brooklyn Museum. (33.675)

figure are painted or modeled on the body of the urn but the head of the figure is modeled on the urn cover. The incision and painting resemble the Marajão style.

On the Rio Napo in eastern Ecuador is still a third site with effigy urns, although in this case the limbs are free modeled as separate appendages. However, the vessels

Fig. 203. Vessel in shape of a woman with incised and painted decorations. Marajão, Brazil. Clay, 8⅜″ high. Collection: American Museum of Natural History. (41.0/1436)

174

Fig. 204. Small vessel covered with finely engraved decorations. Two modeled animal heads protrude from its sides. Marajão, Brazil. Clay, 2½" high. Collection: American Museum of Natural History. (41.1/3988)

are decorated with relief, incision, and black, red, and white painting.

All three of these Amazon River sites are united not only by the concept of effigy urns but also by decorative techniques, colors, and design patterns. There is no evidence for the antiquity of these sites, and the manufacture of effigy urns is known to have persisted into post-European times, since some have been found which are decorated with glass beads. Recent work at Marajão has failed to show that it is very ancient.

The town of Santarem at the mouth of the Tapajós River is apparently built over an ancient burial ground. The local inhabitants have dug out a great variety of ceramic vessels which represent bowls and jars elaborately decorated with modeled lugs and figures. So amazing are the combinations, that the Santarem vessels are often called "tourist" ware, since the intent of the artist seems to have been to startle and catch the eye of the buyer.

The archeological sites of Amazonia cannot be identified with any specific contemporary tribes. However, in the Montaña region, along the eastern slopes of the Andes, the modern Indians make a thin-walled pottery with polychrome designs. The alternating broad and fine lines form figures of conventional animals reminiscent of the earlier Rio Napo and Marajão styles.

Fig. 205. Bowl on stand. The clay vessels of this culture are richly decorated with incised lines and modeled figures in the round. Santarem, Brazil. Clay, 6″ high. Collection: University Museum, Philadelphia. (32-25-182)

Fig. 206. Bottle. This piece, made before the Conquest, strangely resembles a baroque candlestick in all its flamboyance. Santarem, Brazil. Clay, 7″ high. Collection: University Museum, Philadelphia. (34-25-185)

Fig. 207. Vessel in shape of a hunchback with a rattle in one hand and a bag hanging from his shoulder. Only the small animal heads protruding from the bag recall the florid Santarem style, while the figure itself is of monumental simplicity. Santarem, Brazil. Clay, 17″ high. Collection: University Museum, Philadelphia. (L-109-1)

Fig. 208. Three-quarter view of Fig. 207

BIBLIOGRAPHY

THE ANDES

BENNETT, W. C. and BIRD, J. B. Andean culture history, New York, 1949

HAY, C. I. (editor). The Maya and their neighbors, New York, 1940

JAMES, P. E. Latin America, New York, 1942

JOYCE, T. A. South American archaeology, Boston, 1912

KELEMEN, P. Medieval American art, New York, 1943, 2 vols.

STEWARD, J. H. (editor). Handbook of South American Indians, *Bulletin, Bureau of American Ethnology*, 143, 1946, vol. 2

STRONG, W. D. Cross sections of New World prehistory, *Miscellaneous Collection, Smithsonian Institution*, 104, 1943, no. 2

TAX, S. (editor). The civilizations of ancient America, Chicago, 1951

UHLE, M. Kultur und Industrie des Südamerikanischer Völker, Berlin, 1889-90, 2 vols.

THE INCA EMPIRE

BAUDIN, L. L'empire socialiste des Inka, *Traveaux et Mémoires, L'Institut d'Ethnologie*, 5, 1928

JIJÓN Y CAAMAÑO, J. La religión del imperio de los Incas, Quito, 1919

LOCKE, L. L. The ancient quipu or Peruvian knot record, New York, 1923

MARKHAM, C. R. The Incas of Peru, London, 1910

MEANS, P. A. Ancient civilizations of the Andes, New York, 1931

——— Fall of the Inca empire, New York, 1932

MURDOCK, G. P. Our primitive contemporaries, New York, 1934, chap. 14

PRESCOTT, W. H. History of the conquest of Peru, New York, 1847, 2 vols.

ROWE, J. H. Inca culture at the time of the Spanish conquest, *Bulletin, Bureau of American Ethnology*, 143, 1946, vol. 2

THE CENTRAL ANDES

BAESSLER, A. Ancient Peruvian art, Berlin and New York, 1902-03, 4 vols.

BASLER, A. and BRUMMER, E. L'art précolombien, Paris, 1947

BENNETT, W. C. The archeology of the Central Andes, *Bulletin, Bureau of American Ethnology*, 143, 1946, vol. 2

——— (editor). A reappraisal of Peruvian archeology, *Memoir, Society for American Archeology*, 4, 1948

DOERING, H. U. The art of ancient Peru, New York, 1952

HORKHEIMER, H. El Peru prehispánico, Lima, 1950

KROEBER, A. L. Peruvian archeology in 1942, *Publications in Anthropology, Viking Fund*, 4, 1944

LEHMANN, W. and DOERING, H. U. The art of old Peru, New York, 1924

MEAD, C. W. Old civilizations of Inca land, New York, 1924

MUELLE, J. C. and BLAS, C. Muestrario del arte peruano precolombino, *Revista, Museo Nacional de Lima*, 7, 1938

SCHMIDT, M. Kunst und Kultur von Peru, Berlin, 1929

SELER, E. Peruanische Alterthümer, Berlin, 1893

TELLO, J. C. Antiguo Peru, Lima, 1929

——— Origen y desarrollo de las civilizaciones prehistóricas andinas, Lima, 1942

——— Arte antiguo peruano, *Inca*, 2, 1938

WASSERMANN-SAN BLAS, B. J. Cerámicas del antiguo Peru, Buenos Aires, 1938

WILLEY, G. R. Horizon styles and pottery traditions in Peruvian archeology, *American Antiquity*, 11, 1945, pp. 49-56

CRAFTS

CERAMICS

HARCOURT, R. and M. D', La céramique ancienne du Pérou, Paris, 1924

LINNÉ, S. The technique of South American ceramics, Göteborg, 1925

METALLURGY

BAESSLER, A. Altperuanische Metallgeräte, Berlin, 1906

LOTHROP, S. K. Gold and silver from southern Peru and Bolivia, *Journal, Royal Anthropological Institute of Great Britain and Ireland*, 67, 1937, pp. 305-25

——— Inca treasure as depicted by Spanish historians, *Publication Fund, Frederick Webb Hodge Anniversary*, 2, 1938, pp. 1-75

MEAD, C. W. Prehistoric bronze in South America, *Anthropological Papers, American Museum of Natural History*, 12, 1915

NORDENSKIÖLD, E. The copper and bronze ages in South America, Göteborg, 1921

RIVET, P. and ARSANDAUX, H. La métallurgie en Amérique précolombienne, *Traveaux et Mémoires, l'Institut d'Ethnologie*, 39, 1946

ROOT, W. C. The metallurgy of the southern coast of Peru, *American Antiquity*, 15, 1949, pp. 10-37

WEAVING

BENNETT, W. C. and BIRD, J. B. Andean culture history, New York, 1949

CRAWFORD, M. D. C. Peruvian textiles, *Anthropological Papers, American Museum of Natural History*, 12, 1915

HARCOURT, R. D'. Les textiles anciens du Pérou et leurs techniques, Paris, 1934

LEVILLIER, J. Paracas, a contribution to the study of pre-Incaic textiles in ancient Peru, Paris, 1928

MEANS, P. A. Peruvian textiles, New York, 1930

MONTELL, G. Dress and ornaments in ancient Peru, Göteborg, 1929

O'NEALE, L. M. Textiles of the Early Nazca period, *Anthropology Memoirs, Field Museum of Natural History*, 2, 1937, no. 3

———— Textile periods in ancient Peru, *Publications in American Archaeology and Ethnology, University of California*, 39, 1942, no. 2

O'NEALE, L. M. and CLARK, B. J. Textile periods in ancient Peru, *Publications in American Archaeology and Ethnology, University of California*, 40, 1948, no. 4

O'NEALE, L. M. and KROEBER, A. L. Textile periods in ancient Peru, *Publications in American Archaeology and Ethnology, University of California*, 28, 1930, no. 2

STAFFORD, C. E. Paracas embroideries, New York, 1941

YACOVLEFF, E. Arte plumaria entre los antiguos peruanos, *Revista, Museo Nacional de Lima*, 2, 1933

ZIMMERN, N. H. The tapestries of colonial Peru, *Journal, Brooklyn Museum*, 1943-44, pp. 25-52

CENTRAL ANDEAN CULTURES

ORIGINS

BIRD, J. B. Antiquity and migrations of the early inhabitants of Patagonia, *Geographical Review*, 38, 1938, pp. 250-75

———— Preceramic cultures in Chicama and Viru, *Memoirs, Society for American Archeology*, 4, 1948, pp. 21-28

HRDLIČKA, A. Early man in South America, *Bulletin, Bureau of American Ethnology*, 52, 1912

MANGELSDORF, P. C. and REEVES, R. G. The origin of Indian corn and its relatives, *Bulletin, Texas Agricultural Experimental Station*, 574, 1939

SAUER, C. American agricultural origins, *Essays in Anthropology*, Berkeley, 1936, pp. 279-97

SULLIVAN, L. R. and HELLMAN, M. The Punín calvarium, *Anthropological Papers, American Museum of Natural History*, 23, 1925, pp. 309-37

TSCHOPIK, H. Some notes on rock shelter sites near Huancayo, Peru, *American Antiquity*, 12, 1946, pp. 73-80

NORTH COAST

BENNETT, W. C. Archaeology of the north coast of Peru, *Anthropological Papers, American Museum of Natural History*, 37, 1939, part 1

———— The Gallinazo group, *Publications in Anthropology, Yale University*, 43, 1950

FORD, J. A. and WILLEY, G. R. Surface survey of the Viru valley, Peru, *Anthropological Papers, American Museum of Natural History*, 43, 1949, part 1

HOLSTEIN, O. Chan-Chan: Capital of the Great Chimu, *Geographical Review*, 17, 1927, pp. 36-61

KROEBER, A. L. The Uhle pottery collections from Moche, *Publications in American Archaeology and Ethnology, University of California*, 21, 1925, pp. 191-234

———— Ancient pottery from Trujillo, *Anthropology Memoirs, Field Museum of Natural History*, 2, 1926, no. 1

———— The northern coast, *Anthropology Memoirs, Field Museum of Natural History*, 2, 1930, no. 2

LARCO HOYLE, R. Los Mochicas, Lima, 1938-39, 2 vols.

———— Los Cupisniques, Lima, 1941

———— Cultura Salinar, Trujillo, 1944

———— La cultura Virú, Buenos Aires, 1945

———— Cronología arqueológica del norte del Peru, Buenos Aires, 1948

ROWE, J. H. The Kingdom of Chimor, *Acta Americana*, 6, 1948, pp. 26-59

SCHAEDEL, R. P. Major ceremonial and population centers in northern Peru, *Ancient Civilizations of the Americas*, Chicago, 1951, pp. 232-43

STRONG, W. D. and EVANS, C. Cultural stratigraphy in the Viru valley, northern Peru, *Columbia Studies in Archeology and Ethnology*, 4, 1952

CENTRAL COAST

GAYTON, A. H. The Uhle collections from Nievería, *Publications in American Archaeology and Ethnology, University of California*, 21, 1925, no. 8

HARCOURT, RAOUL D'. La céramique de Cajamarquilla-Nievería, *Journal, Société des Américanistes de Paris*, 14, 1922, pp. 107-18

Jijón y Caamaño, J. Maranga, Quito, 1949

Kroeber, A. L. The Uhle pottery collections from Supe, *Publications in American Archaeology and Ethnology, University of California*, 21, 1925, no. 6

——— The Uhle pottery collections from Chancay, *Publications in American Archaeology and Ethnology, University of California*, 21, 1926, no. 7

Reiss, W. and Stübel, A. The necropolis of Ancon in Peru, Berlin, 1880-87, 3 vols.

Strong, W. D. The Uhle pottery collections from Ancon, *Publications in American Archaeology and Ethnology, University of California*, 21, 1925, no. 4

Strong, W. D., Corbett, J. M. and Willey, G. R. Archeological studies in Peru, *Columbia Studies in Archeology and Ethnology*, 1, 1943

Uhle, M. Pachacamac, Philadelphia, 1903

SOUTH COAST

Berthon, P. Etude sur le précolombien du Bas-Pérou, *Nouvelles Archives, Missions Scientifiques et Littéraires*, 4, 1911, pp. 53-122

Carrión Cachot, R. Paracas cultural elements, Lima, 1949

Doering, H. U. Tonplastik aus Nazca, *Ipek*, 2, 1927, pp. 167-75

Gayton, A. H. and Kroeber, A. L. The Uhle pottery collections from Nazca, *Publications in American Archaeology and Ethnology, University of California*, 24, 1927, no. 1

Kroeber, A. L. Cañete valley, *Anthropology Memoirs, Field Museum of Natural History*, 2, 1937, part 4

Kroeber, A. L. and Strong, W. D. The Uhle collections from Chincha, *Publications in American Archaeology and Ethnology, University of California*, 21, 1924, no. 1

——— The Uhle pottery collections from Ica, *Publications in American Archaeology and Ethnology, University of California*, 21, 1924, no. 3

Tello, J. C. Los descubrimientos del Museo de Arqueología Peruana en la península de Paracas, *Proceedings, International Congress of Americanists*, 22, 1926, pp. 679-90

Yacovleff, E. La deidad primitiva de los Nasca, *Revista, Museo Nacional de Lima*, 2, 1932, pp. 103-60

Yacovleff, E. and Muelle, J. C. Una exploración en Cerro Colorado, *Revista, Museo Nacional de Lima*, 2, 1932, pp. 31-59

NORTH HIGHLANDS

Bennett, W. C. Chavín stone carving, *Anthropological Studies, Yale University*, 3, 1942

——— The north highlands of Peru, *Anthropological Papers, American Museum of Natural History*, 39, 1944, part 1

Carrión Cachot, R. La cultura Chavín, *Revista, Museo Nacional de Antropología y Arqueología*, 2, 1948, pp. 99-172

McCown, T. D. Pre-Incaic Huamachuco, *Publications in American Archaeology and Ethnology, University of California*, 39, 1945, no. 4

Reichlen, H. and P. Recherches archéologiques dans les Andes de Cajamarca, *Journal, Société des Américanistes de Paris*, 38, 1949, pp. 137-74

Schaedel, R. P. The Callejón de Huaylas of Peru and its monuments, *Archaeology*, 1, 1948, pp. 198-202

Tello, Julio C. Wira-Kocha, *Inca*, 1, 1923, pp. 92-320.

——— Discovery of the Chavín culture in Peru, *American Antiquity*, 9, 1943, pp. 135-60

Willey, G. R. The Chavín problem: a review and critique, *Southwestern Journal of Anthropology*, 7, 1951, pp. 103-44

CENTRAL HIGHLANDS

Bingham, H. In the wonderland of Peru, *National Geographic*, 24, 1913, pp. 387-573

——— The story of Machu Picchu, *National Geographic*, 27, 1915, pp. 172-216

——— Types of Machu Picchu pottery, *American Anthropologist*, 17, 1915, pp. 257-71

——— Inca land, Boston, 1922

——— Machu Picchu, a citadel of the Incas, New Haven, 1930

Fejos, P. Archaeological explorations in the cordillera Vilcabamba, *Publications in Anthropology, Viking Fund*, 3, 1944

Pardo, L. A. Ruinas precolombinas del Cuzco, Cuzco, 1937

Rowe, J. H. An introduction to the archaeology of Cuzco, *Papers, Peabody Museum, Harvard University*, 27, 1944, no. 2

Valcárcel, L. E. Sajsawaman redescubierto, *Revista, Museo Nacional de Lima*, 3, 1934, pp. 3-36

——— Los trabajos arqueológicos del Cusco, *Revista, Museo Nacional de Lima*, 3, 1934, pp. 211-23

SOUTH HIGHLANDS

Bandelier, A. F. The islands of Titicaca and Koati, New York, 1910

Bennett, W. C. Excavations at Tiahuanaco, *Anthropological Papers, American Museum of Natural History*, 34, 1934, part 3

——— Excavations in Bolivia, *Anthropological Papers, American Museum of Natural History*, 35, 1936, part 4

Kidder, A., Jr. Some early sites in the northern Lake Titicaca basin, *Papers, Peabody Museum, Harvard University*, 27, 1943, no. 1

Posnansky, A. Tihuanacu. The cradle of American man, New York, 1946

Rydén, S. Archaeological researches in the highlands of Bolivia, Göteborg, 1947

STÜBEL, A. and UHLE, M. Die Ruinenstätte von Tiahuanaco, Leipzig, 1892

TSCHOPIK, M. H. Some notes on the archaeology of the department of Puno, Peru, *Papers, Peabody Museum, Harvard University*, 27, 1946, no. 3

VALCÁRCEL, L. Cerámica y litoesculturas de Pukara, *Revista, Museo Nacional de Lima*, 4, 1935, pp. 25-8

THE SOUTH

AMBROSETTI, J. B. Exploraciones arqueológicas en la ciudad prehistórica de "La Paya", Buenos Aires, 1907

BENNETT, W. C., BLEILER, E. F. and SOMMER, F. H. Northwest Argentine archeology, *Publications in Anthropology, Yale University*, 38, 1948

BIRD, J. B. Excavations in northern Chile, *Anthropological Papers, American Museum of Natural History*, 38, 1943, part 4

BOMAN, E. Antiquités de la région andine de la République Argentine et du désert d'Atacama, Paris, 1908, 2 vols.

BREGANTE, O. Ensayo de clasificación de la cerámica del noroeste Argentino, Buenos Aires, 1926

DEBENEDETTI, S. L'ancienne civilisation des Barreales, *Ars Americana*, 2, 1931

LATCHAM, R. E. Arqueología de la región atacameña, Santiago, 1938

MONTELL, G. An archaeological collection from the Río Loa valley, Atacama, *Skrifter, Oslo Etnografiske Museums*, 5, 1926, part 1

RYDÉN, S. Archaeological researches in the department of La Candelaria, *Etnologiska Studier*, 3, 1936

WAGNER, E. R. and D. L. La civilización Chaco-Santiagueña y sus correlaciones con las del viejo y nuevo mundo, Buenos Aires, 1934

THE NORTH

ECUADOR

BENNETT, W. C. Excavations in the Cuenca region, Ecuador, *Publications in Anthropology, Yale University*, 35, 1946

BUSHNELL, G. H. S. The archaeology of the Santa Elena peninsula in southwest Ecuador, Cambridge, 1951

COLLIER, D. The archaeology of Ecuador, *Bulletin, Bureau of American Ethnology*, 143, 1946, vol. 2

COLLIER, D. and MURRA, J. V. Survey and excavations in southern Ecuador, *Anthropological Series, Field Museum of Natural History*, 35, 1943

HARCOURT, RAOUL D'. Archéologie de la province d'Esmeraldas, Equateur, *Journal, Société des Américanistes de Paris*, 35, 1942, pp. 61-200

JIJÓN Y CAAMAÑO, J. Contribución al conocimiento de los aborígenes de la provincia de Imbabura en la República del Ecuador, Madrid, 1914

——— Puruhá: contribución al conocimiento de los aborígenes de la provincia de Chimborazo, Quito, 1927, 2 vols.

ROWE, J. H. The potters' art of Atacames, *Archaeology*, 2, 1949, pp. 31-4

SAVILLE, M. H. The antiquities of Manabí, Ecuador, New York, 1907-10, 2 vols.

——— Archaeological researches on the coast of Esmeraldas, *Proceedings, International Congress of Americanists*, 16, 1909, pp. 331-45

UHLE, M. Las ruinas de Tomebamba, Quito, 1923

VERNEAU, R. and RIVET, P. Ethnographie ancienne de l'Equateur, Paris, 1912-20, 2 vols.

COLOMBIA

BENNETT, W. C. Archeological regions of Colombia: a ceramic survey, *Publications in Anthropology, Yale University*, 30, 1944

BOLLAERT, W. Antiquarian, ethnological and other researches in New Granada, Ecuador, Peru and Chile, London, 1860

BURG, G. Beitrag zur Etnographie Sudkolumbiens auf Grund eigener Forschungen, *Ibero-Amerikanisches Archiv*, 11, 1937-38, pp. 333-75

CREQUI-MONTFORT, G. and RIVET, P. Contribution a l'étude de l'archéologie et de la métallurgie colombiennes, *Journal, Société des Américanistes de Paris*, 11, 1914-19, pp. 525-91

FORD, J. A. Excavations in the vicinity of Cali, Colombia, *Publications in Anthropology, Yale University*, 31, 1944

HERNÁNDEZ DE ALBA, G. Investigaciones arqueológicas en Tierradentro, *Revista de Las Indias*, 2, 1938

——— Colombian archaeology, Bogota, 1941

MASON, J. A. Archaeology of Santa Marta, Colombia, *Anthropological Series, Field Museum of Natural History*, 20, 1931-39, 3 parts

PÉREZ DE BARRADAS, J. Arqueología y antropología precolombinas de Tierra Dentro, Bogota, 1937

——— Arqueología agustiniana, Bogota, 1943

PREUSS, K. TH. Monumentale Vorgeschichtliche Kunst, Göttingen, 1921, 2 vols.

REICHEL-DOLMATOFF, G. and A. Investigaciones arqueológicas en el departamento del Magdalena, 1946-1950, Bogota, 1951

RESTREPO, V. Los Chibchas antes de la conquista española, Bogota, 1895

RIVET, P. La travail de l'or en Colombie, *Ipek*, 2, 1926, pp. 128-41

WASSÉN, H. An archaeological study in the western Colombian cordillera, *Etnologiska Studier*, 2, 1936, pp. 30-67

VENEZUELA

BENNETT, W. C. Excavations at La Mata, Maracay, Venezuela, *Anthropological Papers, American Museum of Natural History*, 36, 1937, part 2

HOWARD, G. D. Excavations at Ronquín, Venezuela, *Publications in Anthropology, Yale University*, 28, 1943

KIDDER, A., JR. The archeology of Venezuela, *Bulletin, Bureau of American Ethnology*, 143, 1948, vol. 4

―――― Archaeology of Northwest Venezuela, *Papers, Peabody Museum, Harvard University*, 26, 1944, no. 1

OSGOOD, C. Excavations at Tocorón, Venezuela, *Publications in Anthropology, Yale University*, 29, 1943

OSGOOD, C. and HOWARD, G. D. An archeological survey of Venezuela, *Publications in Anthropology, Yale University*, 27, 1943

REQUENA, R. Vestigios de la Atlántida, Caracas, 1932

PANAMA

LINNÉ, S. Darien in the past, Göteborg, 1929

LOTHROP, S. K. Coclé, an archaeological study of central Panama, *Memoirs, Peabody Museum, Harvard University*, 7-8, 1937-42, 2 vols.

COSTA RICA

LOTHROP, S. K. Pottery of Costa Rica and Nicaragua, *Contributions, Museum of the American Indian, Heye Foundation*, 8, 1926, 2 vols.

STRONG, W. D. The Archeology of Central America, *Bulletin, Bureau of American Ethnology*, 143, 1948, vol. 4

THE EAST

HOWARD, G. D. Prehistoric ceramic styles in lowland South America, *Publications in Anthropology, Yale University*, 37, 1947

NORDENSKIÖLD, E. L'Archéologie du bassin de l'Amazone, *Ars Americana*, 1, 1930

PALMATARY, H. Tapajó pottery, *Etnologiska Studier*, 8, 1939

―――― The pottery of Marajó island, Brazil, *Transactions, American Philosophical Society*, 39, 1949, part 3

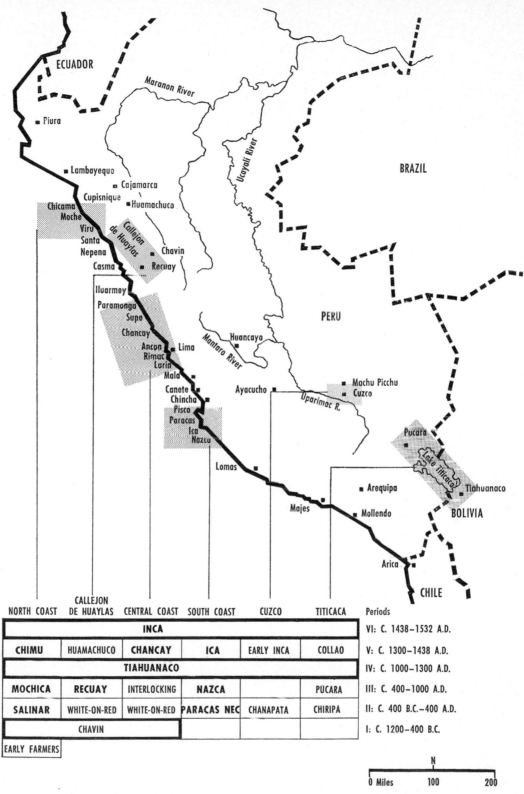

NORTH COAST	CALLEJON DE HUAYLAS	CENTRAL COAST	SOUTH COAST	CUZCO	TITICACA	Periods
INCA						VI: C. 1438–1532 A.D.
CHIMU	HUAMACHUCO	CHANCAY	ICA	EARLY INCA	COLLAO	V: C. 1300–1438 A.D.
TIAHUANACO						IV: C. 1000–1300 A.D.
MOCHICA	RECUAY	INTERLOCKING	NAZCA		PUCARA	III: C. 400–1000 A.D.
SALINAR	WHITE-ON-RED	WHITE-ON-RED	PARACAS NEC	CHANAPATA	CHIRIPA	II: C. 400 B.C.–400 A.D.
CHAVIN						I: C. 1200–400 B.C.
EARLY FARMERS						

N
0 Miles   100   200

ANCIENT INDIAN CULTURES OF THE CENTRAL ANDES
REGIONAL AND TIME DIVISIONS

185

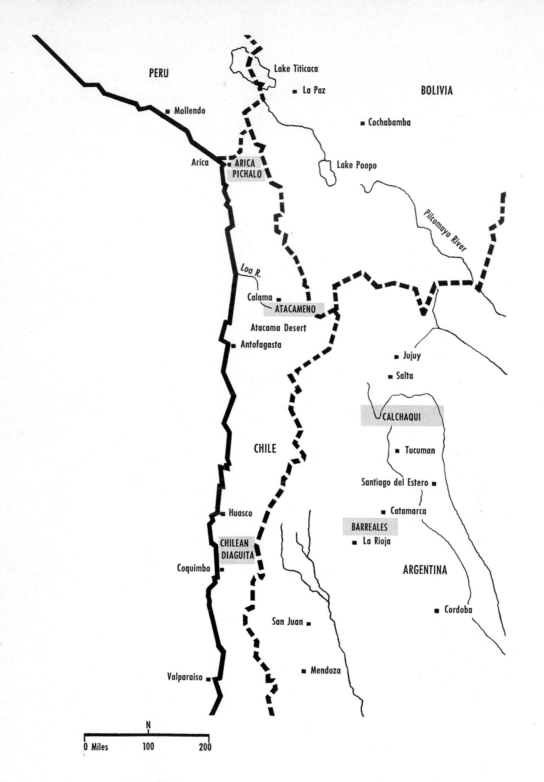

ANCIENT INDIAN CULTURES OF THE SOUTHERN ANDES

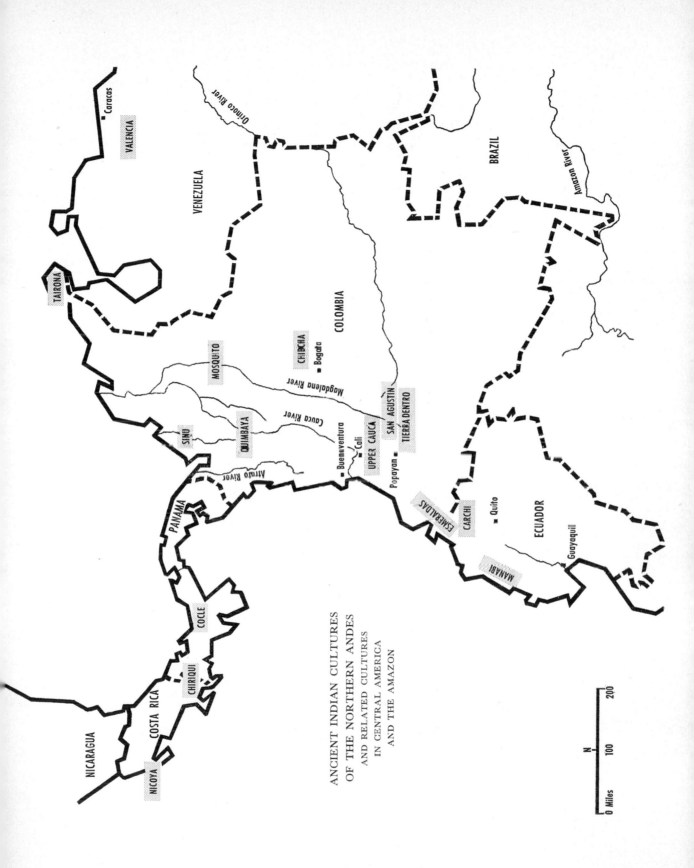

ANCIENT INDIAN CULTURES
OF THE NORTHERN ANDES
AND RELATED CULTURES
IN CENTRAL AMERICA
AND THE AMAZON

NICARAGUA

NICOYA

COSTA RICA

CHIRIQUI

COCLE

PANAMA

Atrato River

SINÚ

QUIMBAYA

MOSQUITO

TAIRONA

VALENCIA

Caracas

VENEZUELA

Orinoco River

COLOMBIA

BRAZIL

Amazon River

CHIBCHA

Bogotá

Magdalena River

Cauca River

Buenaventura

Cali

UPPER CAUCA

SAN AGUSTIN

TIERRA DENTRO

Popayan

ESMERALDAS

CARCH

Quito

MANABI

Guayaquil

ECUADOR

N

0 Miles   100   200

This book has been printed in January, 1954, for the Trustees of the Museum of Modern Art by the Plantin Press, New York. The color plates were printed by Thames and Hudson, London and The John P. Smith Co., Rochester, New York.

Southern Central America

Nicoya
San Jose
PANAMA
COSTA RICA

Buenaventura

The Northern Andes

Santa Marta
Valencia · Caracas
VENEZUELA

Orinoco River

Cauca River
Magdalena River
· Bogota

COLOMBIA

· Quito
Napo R.
ECUADOR

Maranon R.

Ucayali R.

Amazon Region

Amazon River   MARAJAO

Mirakanguera

· Santarem

Madeira River

Tapajoz River

The Central Andes

· Trujillo

· Lima
PERU

· Cuzco

Lake Titicaca
· La Pa...
BOLIVIA

BRAZIL

The Southern Andes

ATACAMA
CHILE

ARGENTINA

Valparaiso · · Santiago

Buenos Aires   · Plata River